I'm going to walk you
through 500 years and
show you how God is
literally screaming
at the world,
"I'M COMING SOON!"

FOUR BLOOD MOONS
OF 2014-2015

What will occur in the 2014-2015 time period?

April 15, 2014
First Day of
Passover

Oct. 8, 2014
First Day of
Sukkoth

April 4, 2015
First Day of
Passover

Sept. 28, 2015
First Day of
Sukkoth

The next Four Blood Moons begins in April 2014 and ends in September 2015. History is getting ready to change forever!

ARE YOU READY?

And I will show wonders in the heavens and in the earth: blood and fire and pillars of smoke. The sun shall be turned into darkness, and the moon into blood, before the coming of the great and awesome day of the Lord.

JOEL 2:30-31 NKJV

SOMETHING IS
ABOUT TO CHANGE

JHM.ORG

I believe the heavens
are God's billboard. That
He has been sending
signals to planet Earth
and we just haven't been
picking them up.

FOUR BLOOD MOONS
OF 1492

1492
The Spanish
Inquisition

April 2, 1493
Passover

Sept. 25, 1493
Sukkoth

March 22, 1494
Passover

Sept. 15, 1494
Sukkoth

The Four Blood Moons of 1492 announced the Edict of Expulsion for the Jewish people from Spain by King Ferdinand and Queen Isabella. The week of April 29, 1492, the Jews of Spain were given 14 days to leave Spain forever. All of their properties left behind went to the state which was controlled by the Roman Church.

The Edict of Expulsion was the crescendo of suffering for the Jewish people. They had endured the Spanish Inquisition led by Cardinal Torquemada. During this Inquisition Jews were burned alive at the stake for refusing to convert to Catholicism; others were tortured on a rack producing excruciating suffering. With the Edict of Expulsion they lost their homes and many gave their children to Christian families to raise them to guarantee their physical survival.

The long night of tears ended in triumph when Christopher Columbus, funded by Jewish money and maps, discovered America on October 12, 1492 which became the haven of rest for the Jewish people around the world.

FOUR
BLOOD
MOONS

SOMETHING IS ABOUT TO CHANGE

FOUR BLOOD MOONS
OF 1948

The Four Blood Moons of 1948 were preceded by the tears of terror caused by the Holocaust. It was an unspeakable time of suffering by the Jewish people. The tears of the Holocaust were ended by the triumph of the birth of the State of Israel.

The Four Blood Moons of 1948 was the year the State of Israel was re-born after almost 2000 years of the Diaspora. The mighty right hand of God gathered the Jewish exiles from the nations of the world and brought them home to the land of covenant as prophesied by the Old Testament Prophets.

There is no greater miracle in human history than May 14, 1948 when David Ben Gurion rushed down Rothchild Boulevard in Tel Aviv and stopped in front of the art museum.

Ben Gurion quickly bounded up the steps and precisely at 4 o'clock, he stepped to the podium and read the words that gave birth to the modern state of Israel. Eleven minutes later Harry Truman recognized the State of Israel and world history was made. God sent us a signal that history was about to change forever...and it did.

FOUR BLOOD MOONS
OF 1967

1967
The Six-Day War

April 24, 1967
First Day of Passover

Oct. 18, 1967
First Day of Sukkoth

April 13, 1968
First Day of Passover

Oct. 6, 1968
First Day of Sukkoth

The Four Blood Moons of 1967 is when the city of Jerusalem was joined to the State of Israel. After Israel was declared a state in 1948, the city of Jerusalem was controlled by Jordan.

In the war of 1967 the city of Jerusalem was captured by the Israel Defense Forces and Jews were praying at the Western Wall for the first time in 2000 years.

Jerusalem is unlike any city in the world! Jerusalem is the city of God. Jerusalem is where Jeremiah and Isaiah wrote principles of righteousness that became the moral and spiritual foundations of Western civilization.

Jerusalem is the city that King David captured from the Jebusites 3000 years ago. Jerusalem is where Jesus Christ was crucified for the sins of the world. Jerusalem is where He will return to rule a global kingdom that shall never end. The unification of Jerusalem with the State of Israel was prophetically an earth shaking event. History was being changed forever. God sent us the announcement in the Four Blood Moons.

There will be signs in the sun, in the moon, and in the stars ... Now when these things begin to happen, look up and lift up your heads, because your redemption draws near."

— Luke 21:25a, 28

FOUR
BLOOD
MOONS

COMPANION
STUDY GUIDE AND JOURNAL

Library of Congress Control Number: 2014941948

Published in association with Ted Squires Agency, Nashville, Tennessee

For foreign and subsidiary rights, contact rights@worthypublishing.com

ISBN: 978-1-61795-387-3

Cover Design: Christopher Tobias
Interior Design and Typesetting: Kimberly Sagmiller, FudgeCreative.com

Printed in the United States of America
14 15 16 17 LBM 8 7 6 5 4 3 2 1

FOUR BLOOD M●ONS

COMPANION
STUDY GUIDE AND JOURNAL

JOHN HAGEE

WORTHY°
PUBLISHING

It gives me great pleasure to dedicate this *Four Blood Moons Companion Study Guide and Journal* to my television partners across the nation and around the world who have faithfully supported this ministry for almost forty years.

Together, we have preached "All the Gospel to All the World!" Tens of thousands of souls have been saved, broken hearts have been mended, shattered marriages renewed, sick bodies healed, and countless legions liberated by the power of the gospel of Jesus Christ.

Blessings and peace to you, my dear partners, who will be recognized and rewarded in heaven by a loving God who has recorded every gift and every soul.

CONTENTS

And there will be signs in the sun, in the moon,
and in the stars; and on the earth distress of nations . . .
Then they will see the Son of Man coming in a cloud
with power and great glory. *Now when these things
begin to happen, look up and lift up your heads,
because your redemption draws near.*

—LUKE 21:25, 27-28

A Word from Pastor Hagee

Something big is about to happen—are you ready?

In *Four Blood Moons: Something Is about to Change,* I described how my friend, Pastor Mark Biltz, challenged me with a question that changed my life: "Have you ever considered the sun, moon, and stars in the study of prophecy?"

Intrigued by this question, I took Pastor Mark's challenge and started studying Scripture alongside NASA's scientific records of the movements of the sun, moon, and stars. The results were astounding—and undeniable. God has clearly been using the heavens as His high-definition billboard to announce significant events on the earth, events that He set into motion before the foundation of the world and marked out in advance through the movements and orbits of heavenly bodies.

As I continued to study astronomical events alongside biblical prophecy and world history, I was astounded by how Scripture, science, and significant historical events continued to line up together. The reality of God's supernatural involvement in the heavens—from creation, through the Old and New Testaments, and continuing throughout church history to the present day—became crystal clear. I sensed God urging me to write *Four Blood Moons* to share His message with the world, to prepare Christians for something big that He is about to do, something He is announcing in the sky for the world to see in the coming Four Blood Moons.

Since the publication of *Four Blood Moons* in 2013, I have been flooded with letters, e-mails, and phone calls from people who have read the book and are eager to learn more. They have joined me in exploring deeper into the truth of God's Word alongside the facts of science and history—and they, too, are discovering the prophetic significance of studying the Word of God in light of current astronomical and world events. They want to be prepared for what is coming as well as support God's covenant people, the nation of Israel, like never before.

I have written this companion study guide and journal for those of you who want to go further in your study of biblical prophecy—who desire to learn more about the coming Four Blood Moons and who want to learn practical ways that the Body of Christ can prepare for the coming day of the Lord. It is my prayer that God will speak to your heart as you read *Four Blood Moons* and go through this companion study guide and journal, revealing to you the things He is announcing right now through the sun, moon, and stars.

Heavenly Father,

In the authority of Jesus' name, as we begin this deeper journey into the Four Blood Moons, we ask that You reveal the truth of Your Word to us. May we walk in the confidence that the Lord is the God of Abraham, Isaac and Jacob, that He is the Creator of heaven and earth and is in control of all things. Keep us in the hollow of Your hand and let no man remove us.

In the blessed name of the Father, the Son, and the Holy Spirit we pray, amen.

How to Use This Companion Study Guide
and Journal

Welcome to the companion study guide and journal to *Four Blood Moons: Something Is about to Change,* by Pastor John Hagee. This companion resource is written for those who are interested in the 2014–15 series of Four Blood Moons and who want to go deeper in their understanding of what these astronomical events mean for the nation of Israel—and for the world.

Everyone reading the *Four Blood Moons Companion Study Guide and Journal* should first read the *Four Blood Moons* book. This will greatly enhance your experience of the study questions and bonus material. To reinforce the integration of this companion resource with the *Four Blood Moons* book, this study guide features several direct quotes from *Four Blood Moons*. Direct quotes from the book are set in italics, followed by the corresponding page number of *Four Blood Moons* cited in parentheses after the quote, for easy reference.

The design of *Four Blood Moons Companion Study Guide and Journal* enables this resource to be used effectively by individuals or by groups. The material is divided into two sections. Part 1 is an eight-week study guide that contains insights, reflections, and discussion questions to guide you through the sixteen chapters of the *Four Blood Moons* book and help you apply what you have learned.

For those who want to dig even deeper, part 2 contains bonus content that provides more detailed teaching about topics that are mentioned in *Four Blood Moons*. Readers can either use part 2 in conjunction with the eight-week study, as directed in each week's study session, or read these chapters separately to discover further insights on these intriguing subjects.

How to Use Part 1

Following are some suggested steps for getting the most out of part 1 as an eight-week study guide for individual or group use.

Individual Use

- Begin each study session with prayer, asking God to give you insight and wisdom.
- Turn to the opening page of that week's session and reflect on the featured quote from *Four Blood Moons*.
- Read back through the assigned chapters from *Four Blood Moons*. (Most of the sessions cover two chapters of the book.) For the fullest experience of this study guide and journal, reread the *Four Blood Moons* chapters in their entirety.
- Make sure you have your Bible, a pen, and a notebook before you begin the study questions.
- Read and underline in your Bible the "Key Verse" listed for that week's session.
- Read and reflect on the "Key Passage from *Four Blood Moons*." Underline any words or phrases in the passage that stand out to you.
- Take your time and read through the "Questions for Personal Study" for each session. Don't rush. Take the time you need to think through the questions, quotes from *Four Blood Moons*, and word and topical studies. Answer each question honestly and prayerfully.

- Write down your responses in the space provided. Don't be shy about writing in this book! This is intended to be an interactive tool to help you experience the truths of God's Word. If you need more room, write additional insights or reflections in a separate notebook.

- Look up all the Scripture references given. Read them in context. Allow the Holy Spirit to speak to you through the reading of His Word.

- Read through the "Questions for Group Discussion" and think through your answers. Jot down any thought-provoking insights in the spaces provided in this journal.

- Close your week of study with prayer, using the words of the suggested prayer at the end of each session or your own.

- Step up and speak out about what you have learned in that week's session by following through on the suggestions in the "Take Action" section. You might want to check off each item that you apply, as motivation to live out what you are learning.

- After you have completed all eight sessions of the study contained in part 1, consider asking someone else to do this study with you. Perhaps you could even organize and lead a study group through the questions you have answered and applied.

STUDY GROUPS

- If you are leading a study group, ensure that each member of the group obtains a copy of *Four Blood Moons* prior to the study. Direct members to read the book before the study begins, if possible, for the fullest experience of this companion study guide and journal. Ask them to bring their copy of *Four Blood Moons* to each study session, so they can refer to the content and make notes in their books as they learn new insights.

- Prepare in advance to lead the discussion each week. Several days before the study session, set aside some time to read through the session's assigned chapters in *Four Blood Moons*. Do the "Questions for Personal Study" for your own benefit and insight. Then answer and review the "Questions for Group Discussion" that you will be facilitating in the group session. Don't rush. Take the time you need to think through each question and answer honestly and prayerfully.

- If you are able, you may want to work a couple of lessons ahead to get an idea of the overall direction of the study.

- When your group gets together, begin each study session with prayer, asking God to give you wisdom as you lead—and to give the members wisdom as they participate and learn.

- Pass out Bibles and pens to anyone in the study who needs these tools.

- Turn to the opening page of that week's session and read aloud the featured quote from *Four Blood Moons*.

- Ask someone in the group to look up that week's "Key Verse" and read it aloud.

- Read aloud the "Key Passage from *Four Blood Moons*."

- Guide the group through the "Questions for Group Discussion" for that week's session.

- If you don't get to discuss a particular question during your group session, remind members that they can continue to do individual study at home and then share their insights with the group the following week.

- Affirm each person who participates in the discussion, especially if the question is personal, revealing, or comes from a person who is usually quiet.
- Keep the discussion on topic. If someone's answer veers off subject, bring the study back to the topic at hand with gentle reminders such as, "That's an interesting perspective. I'd love to talk about it more with you after the session."
- Give everyone a chance to participate. If someone continually dominates the group discussion, open up the opportunity for others to participate by kindly saying something such as, "I'm grateful for the very valuable contributions you have made to our study so far. Now let's hear from someone else."
- Encourage group members to write down any insights they learn during the group discussion in the space provided on these pages. Remember, this companion study guide and journal is designed to be an interactive tool to help you experience the truths of God's Word.
- Close each group session in prayer. You are welcome to pray spontaneously, or you can use the words of the suggested prayer printed at the end of each week's session.
- Urge the group members to step up and speak out about what they have learned by doing something from the "Take Action" section. For weeks two through eight, ask members what "Take Action" steps they have completed so far. When appropriate, brainstorm ways you can do some of these practical applications together as a group.

How to Use Part 2

Part 2 contains bonus content that will enhance your understanding of the Four Blood Moons. These chapters will equip you to dig deeper into a biblical understanding of prophetic events and how they relate to the nation of Israel—and to us.

In part 2, you will explore subjects such as what the Bible says about astronomical events, how the Jewish feasts relate to biblical prophecy, more detailed information on the end times, and why Christians should support Israel. Also featured are "Frequently Asked Questions about *Four Blood Moons*," which will be of interest to anyone who has read the *Four Blood Moons* book.

Each of the eight study sessions in part 1 suggests a corresponding chapter in part 2 that can be read and discussed in conjunction with that week's session. Or readers can choose to read the chapters of part 2 separately from the study. No matter how you choose to read part 2, you will discover fascinating insights and details on various subjects covered in *Four Blood Moons*.

Every reader should pay careful attention to the last section of the book: "Are You Ready?" This section contains a simple overview of the biblical plan of salvation to use for yourself or share with loved ones. The time is close—we need to be ready!

We pray that the *Four Blood Moons Companion Study Guide and Journal* will be an effective resource to educate and equip this entire generation of Christians to pay attention to God's signs in the heavens and look up—our redemption draws near!

PART ONE

⅃

EXAMINING THE FOUR BLOOD MOONS

Eight-Week Study Guide for Individual or Group Use

WEEK 1:

Does God Speak through the Heavens?

⚬

STUDY OF CHAPTER 1 IN *FOUR BLOOD MOONS*

....

The history of the world is about to change forever,
and God is sending us messages on His high-definition
billboard by speaking to us in the heavens—using the
Four Blood Moons; the question is . . . are we listening?

(*Four Blood Moons*, chapter 1)

....

Prepare for Week 1

- Read chapter 1, "Signs in the Heavens," in *Four Blood Moons.*
- *Optional:* Watch "The Coming Four Blood Moons: Something Is about to Change, part 1" sermon by Pastor John Hagee on YouTube.

KEY VERSE

I will show wonders in the heavens and in the earth:

Blood and fire and pillars of smoke.

The sun shall be turned into darkness,

And the moon into blood,

Before the coming of the great and awesome day of the LORD.

—JOEL 2:30–31

KEY PASSAGE FROM *FOUR BLOOD MOONS*

Does God use the sun, moon, and stars to communicate with us? Does He use the heavens as His own personal, high-definition billboard to announce things to come?

The answer is yes.

—*Four Blood Moons*, chapter 1

⚛

⚜ QUESTIONS FOR PERSONAL STUDY ⚜

CHAPTER 1: SIGNS IN THE HEAVENS

King David said, "You will arise and have compassion on Zion, for it is time to show favor to her; the appointed time has come" (Psalm 102:13 NIV). . . . The appointed time is now! (4)

Zion

The word *Zion* comes from a Semitic root related to a mountaintop fortress. It first appears in 2 Samuel 5:7, which equates "the stronghold of Zion" with the "City of David." Mount Zion is a hill in Jerusalem, often associated with the dwelling place of God. Throughout Scripture, especially in psalms and prophecies, the term *Zion* refers to the city of Jerusalem, and by extension, all of Israel. (See Psalm 2:6; 9:11–12; Isaiah 1:8; 3:16; 2 Kings 19:21; Lamentations 2:10; 4:2.)[1]

• What does it mean to "have compassion on Zion"? In Psalm 102:13, do you think King David is referring to feelings or actions? Why?

WHY SHOULD WE SUPPORT ISRAEL?

If we are to correctly understand heavenly signs and wonders, it's imperative we grasp the full scope of Scripture and history. (5)

Let's look at the five biblical reasons Christians should support the nation of Israel and the Jewish people, listed on pages 5–12 of *Four Blood Moons.*

1. God Promises to Bless Those Who Bless Israel

God's promise is a fact: "I will bless those who bless you" (Genesis 12:3). (7)

- Read Genesis 12:1–3. This is God's pledge to Abraham and the Jewish people for all generations. In the space below, list God's specific promises to Abraham that you observe in these verses, especially those in verse 3.

- In what specific ways has God "blessed" those who "bless Israel"? Look up Luke 7:1–5 and Acts 10:22. List below the two Gentiles and the blessings they received for showing favor to the Jewish people.

    1.

    2.

- What other Gentiles (e.g., biblical characters, historical figures, political leaders, etc.) did practical acts of kindness to bless the Jewish people—and received God's blessing in return? (For ideas, read Genesis 20:17–18 and Genesis 41:46–47.)

2. We Are Commanded to Pray for the Peace of Jerusalem

Praying for the peace of Jerusalem is not a request—it's a command! (7)

- Read Psalm 122:6–7. According to this passage, what specific requests are we commanded to pray for the city of Jerusalem?

- Read Isaiah 9:6–7 and Luke 1:32–33.What do you learn about Jesus' relationship to Jerusalem from these verses? How is Jerusalem connected to His kingdom?

3. **We Are Commanded to Be Watchmen on the Walls of Israel**
We are commanded . . . to speak up and defend Israel and the Jewish people when they are slandered, attacked by their enemies, and are subjected to any callous act of anti-Semitism. (8)

- Read Isaiah 62:1, 6–7. What is the role of watchmen on the walls? What are they watching for?

Watchmen on the Walls

In the ancient world, a "watchman" was a guard or sentinel stationed on top of the city walls, carefully monitoring the actions of the townspeople and anyone who approached the city walls. As the first line of defense against invaders, the watchman was critical to the city's survival. If he spotted a threat, he would sound an alarm and the town would shut its gates and prepare for battle. (See Ezekiel 3:17–19; 33:6–7; Job 27:18; 2 Samuel 18:24–27.)[2]

- In verses 6–7, the watchmen are urged to "not rest" and "not keep silent." Why is this continual watching and speaking out necessary? What could happen if the watchmen were sleeping or silent?

- How does the role of watchmen in the ancient world relate to Christians' role toward Israel today? In what specific ways can we be "watchmen" for the nation of Israel?

4. We Are Commanded to Minister to Israel in Material Things

If you take away the Jewish contribution to Christianity, there would be no Christianity. (10)

- Read Romans 15:27. What "spiritual things" have Christians received from the Jewish people? List as many as you can think of in the space below. (For ideas, see the list on page 9 of *Four Blood Moons.*)

- Read John 4:22. What did Jesus mean when He said, "for salvation is of the Jews"? In what ways does a Christian's salvation come through the Jewish people?

- What are some of the differences between historic Christianity (specifically, the harm inflicted by religious institutions during church history, including the Crusades and Inquisition) and the teachings of Jesus Christ?

5. Jesus Entreated the Church to Support Israel

We should support Israel and the Jewish people because it was Jesus' final request to His church. (10)

- Read Matthew 25:40. How does Jesus connect the Jewish people with Himself in this verse? How do our actions toward the Jews affect Jesus?

"My Brethren"

....

Jesus never called any Gentiles "brethren" until after the cross. Before the cross, Gentiles were outside the covenants of Israel, without God and without hope, of all men most miserable. (See Ephesians 2:12; 1 Corinthians 15:19.) All biblical references to "brethren" prior to the death of Christ refer specifically to the Jewish people.

....

• Read Matthew 5:16 and Matthew 25:34–36. What do these verses tell us about the consequences of our actions (or lack of actions) toward the Jewish people?

My mind went back to Pastor Mark's question: "Have you considered the sun, moon, and stars in the study of prophecy?" Having studied the Bible for fifty-four years and authored numerous books on the subject of prophecy, my mind is a database of prophetic Scripture. Genesis 1:14 came to my mind, which declares that God created the sun, moon, and stars (signals) in the heavens. (17)

ASTRONOMY VERSUS ASTROLOGY

In this book, our discussion of the stars and moon in biblical prophecy is based on the Word of God, history, and the science of astronomy—and never refers to astrology. (18)

• Look up the definitions of *astronomy* and *astrology*. Write the definitions below:

Astronomy:

Astrology:

- What are the differences between these two fields of study? Which one is based on science, and which one is based on human interpretation and imagination?

- Read Romans 1:20–21 and Exodus 20:4. What is God's attitude toward those who try to find guidance for their lives from created things, rather than from their Creator?

- The Bible condemns the practice of astrology as an act of sorcery and divination, which is strongly associated with witchcraft and the occult. Read Isaiah 47:13–14. What does God say will be the consequences for those who practice astrology?

- Should Christians read their daily horoscope? In what ways are horoscopes—the use of the movements of planets and stars to "read into" a person's life and predict his or her future—a form of fortune-telling? Where should Christians turn if they want to know about future events?

For more information on astronomy versus astrology, turn to part 2 of this study guide and read chapter 9: "What Does the Bible Say about Astronomy versus Astrology?"

GOD'S HIGH-DEFINITION BILLBOARD
What do all these prophecies have in common? They all involve specific signs in the heavens preceding coming global events! (20)

- Read Joel 2:30–31 and compare it to Acts 2:19–20. In the space provided, list below the five specific astronomical "wonders"

God says He will show us in the heavens and earth before the "great and awesome day of the Lord."

    1.

    2.

    3.

    4.

    5.

- Exactly how long before Jesus' Second Coming will we see these signs in heaven and on earth? Read Matthew 24:36. What does this verse say about anyone who claims to know the "day and hour" of the Second Coming?

- Read Luke 21:25, 28 and Matthew 24:29–30. What do these two prophecies have in common?

- Even though the Bible says we cannot set a day and time of Jesus' physical return to planet earth, will those who understand the Bible be able to determine the approximate time of His Second Coming? Why or why not?

God uses the sun, moon, and stars as signals to mankind. He uses the heavens as His divine billboard announcing coming events. (20)

- Read Genesis 1:14 and write out below God's purpose for creating the sun, moon, and stars, as stated in this verse.

"Signals"

The Hebrew word for "sign" in Genesis 1:14 is *owth*, which also translates as "signals." In other places in Scripture, this same word is translated "banner," "pledge," or "witness." (See Numbers 2:2; Joshua 2:12; Job 21:29.) God clearly intends the sun, moon, and stars to be beacons announcing His supernatural work on the earth![3]

SIGNS OVER RUSSIA AND IN THE SUN

Signs in the heavens are coming to the enemies of Israel! (23)

- In February 2013, a fiery meteor exploded over Russia, causing shockwaves that injured hundreds of people and damaged thousands of homes. Read the description of this meteor on page 21 of *Four Blood Moons*. In what ways could this astronomical event be considered a "sign from heaven"?

- Read Joshua 10:11. Do you see any possible connection between the "great hailstones" hurled by God in these verses and unusual astronomical phenomena such as the meteor that crashed over Russia?

- Read Ezekiel 38:22–23 and Revelation 8:8–11 to discover how God will use stones from the heavens as weapons of war in the future. What is God's purpose in hurling these stones, as noted in Ezekiel 38:23? Write it out below.

- Recently, scientists have expressed concern over giant solar eruptions. Read the description of these solar flares on pages

23–24 of *Four Blood Moons*. What consequences could a large solar flare have on our current technology?

Signs in the Sun vs. Signs in the Moon

According to Jewish rabbinical scholars:

- A *lunar* eclipse is a signal of God's coming judgment to *Israel*.
- A *solar* eclipse is a signal of coming judgment to the *Gentile nations*.
- When a *solar eclipse* occurs in the center of a series of four *lunar eclipses*, as will happen in the Tetrad of Four Blood Moons in 2014–15, it is a warning to the whole world that something devastating is going to happen!

As you conclude this week's study, read Psalm 19:1–4 aloud:

The heavens declare the glory of God;
    the skies proclaim the work of his hands.
Day after day they pour forth speech;
    night after night they reveal knowledge.
They have no speech, they use no words;
    no sound is heard from them.
Yet their voice goes out into all the earth,
    their words to the ends of the world. (NIV)

- Based on your study of the sun, moon, and stars so far, what is significant to you about the verses above? Underline the words that stand out to you. God is speaking to you through the heavens—are you listening?

• QUESTIONS FOR GROUP DISCUSSION •

• How would you personally answer Pastor Mark's question: "Have you ever considered the sun, moon, and stars in the study of prophecy?" Be honest. Discuss as a group: what do you hope to learn as a result of your study of *Four Blood Moons*?

• How did you respond to the list of five reasons Christians should support the nation of Israel and the Jewish people? In what ways did your study this week show you the importance of supporting Israel? What new insights did you learn? In what ways were you challenged to become more involved in praying for and taking action in support of Israel?

• Discuss the differences between astronomy and astrology that you learned this week. What was your reaction to the Bible's strong warnings against astrology? For further reference, discuss any insights you learned by reading chapter 9 of this study guide: "What Does the Bible Say about Astronomy versus Astrology?"

• The Bible is clear that only God knows the exact time of Jesus' Second Coming (Matthew 24:36). How do you reconcile that verse with Luke 21:25, 28, in which Jesus describes future celestial signs and tells us, "When these things begin to happen, look up and lift up your heads, because your redemption draws near"? What is the difference between predicting a specific date for Jesus' return and recognizing the "signs of the time" of Jesus' Second Coming? Is either approach biblical? Why or why not?

Prayer

Heavenly Father, we pray for the peace of Jerusalem. May they prosper who love You. Show us how we can be "watchmen on the walls" to stand up and speak out for our Jewish brothers and sisters. As we look to the heavens and see our redemption drawing near, we ask You to give us wisdom as we study, eyes to see and ears to hear what You are announcing to the entire world in sun, moon, and stars. In the name of Jesus we pray, amen.

Take Action

- Go to BibleGateway.com and do a keyword study on "Zion." What do you learn from these Bible verses about God's relationship with the Jewish people and this particular location?

- Considering what you learned this week about astronomy versus astrology, are there any habits in your life (such as reading your daily horoscope) that you need to change? If so, confess it to God and commit to walking in the light of God's truth in this area, starting today.

- *Stop talking about how you* feel . . . *and start taking* action *by showing practical acts of kindness toward God's chosen people* (12). Seek out specific, practical ways you can be a "watchman on the wall" to support the Jewish people, such as joining pro-Israel organizations or sending letters and e-mails to your congressmen and representatives to stand strong in your support of Israel.

WEEK 2:
Signs and Stars

❧

STUDY OF CHAPTERS 2–3 IN *FOUR BLOOD MOONS*

The sun, moon, and stars *are unmistakably connected to Israel and biblical prophecy*—and *that* connection inspired this book. God will use them to light up the heavens with an *urgent, top-priority message* for all mankind.

What is God saying to us?

How does the past hold the secret to the future?

What is about to happen on planet earth?

Everything is about to change . . . forever!

(*Four Blood Moons*, chapter 2)

Prepare for Week 2

- Read chapter 2, "The Star in the East," in *Four Blood Moons.*
- Read chapter 3, "Warning Comes before Judgment," in *Four Blood Moons.*

KEY VERSE

In the beginning God created the heavens and the earth. . . . Then God said, "Let there be lights in the firmament of the heavens to divide the day from the night; and let them be for signs and seasons, and for days and years; and let them be for lights in the firmament of the heavens to give light on the earth"; and it was so. Then God made two great lights: the greater light to rule the day, and the lesser light to rule the night. He made the stars also. God set them in the firmament of the heavens to give light on the earth, and to rule over the day and over the night, and to divide the light from the darkness. And God saw that it was good.

—GENESIS 1:1, 14–18

KEY PASSAGE FROM *FOUR BLOOD MOONS*

The [biblical] accounts prove beyond a shadow of a doubt that God has absolute control of the sun, moon, and stars. He has used them in the past to send signals to humanity that something big was about to happen. The heavens are still God's billboard that sends signals to us today—but are we watching for them?

—*Four Blood Moons*, chapter 2

• QUESTIONS FOR PERSONAL STUDY •

CHAPTER 2: THE STAR IN THE EAST

I began my study of the signs in the heavens with one of the most controversial verses in the Bible: "In the beginning God created the heavens and the earth" (Genesis 1:1). (28)

Created

....

The Hebrew word translated "created" in Genesis 1:1 is *bara*, which means "to make from nothing." God didn't come to an established earth and stir some primordial soup that was already here. Instead, He made the entire universe out of *nothing![1]*

....

IN THE BEGINNING . . .

If you don't believe Genesis 1:1, you have no solid foundation to believe the rest of Scripture. (30)

- Read Genesis 1:1. Why is this verse controversial in our society today?

- Why is believing Genesis 1:1—the truth that God created the heavens and the earth—absolutely essential for every Christian? If Genesis 1:1 is not true, what implications would that have for believers? If we can't trust Genesis 1:1, what else can we not trust?

GOD'S CONTROL OVER THE HEAVENS

What is the Bible's evidence that God totally controls the sun, moon, and stars? (31)

- Read Joshua 10:1–13. How does this historical event demonstrate God's total control over the sun?

- Read 2 Kings 20:8–11. What sign did God give King Hezekiah in answer to his prayer, and to show His supernatural and absolute control over the movement of the sun?

- How do the events of 2 Kings 20:8–11 and Joshua 10:1–13 coordinate together in relation to the solar clock? (If you need a hint, read page 34 of *Four Blood Moons*.) How does this again show us God's sovereignty over the heavens?

WISE MEN FOLLOWED THE STAR

The wise men understood the meaning of Micah's prophecy. (36)

- Read Micah 5:2. Who is "the One to be Ruler in Israel" described in this verse? Where does Micah say this Ruler would be born?

- Read Matthew 2:1–10. In the space below, write what the wise men *did* in response to seeing the star (see especially verses 2, 9, and 10):

- The Bible tells us that the wise men paid attention to the sun, moon, and stars—and they took action when they saw the signal God placed in the heavens to lead them to Jesus. What does this tell us about how we should respond to God's heavenly billboard today?

Signs in the Sun, Moon, and Stars

Did Jesus speak about the signs in the heavens and on the earth? Absolutely! (39)

- Read Matthew 24:3. What questions did the disciples ask Jesus?

- Read Matthew 24:29–30. What astronomical occurrences did Jesus tell His disciples to watch for prior to His Second Coming?

- According to Matthew 24:33, when those heavenly signs occur, what will they be announcing? (The New American Standard Bible gives a clearer answer to this, if you need help.)

For more biblical evidence that God controls the heavens, turn to part 2 of this study guide and read chapter 10: "Are There Other Biblical Prophecies Involving the Sun, Moon, and Stars?"

Eureka!

This message from God is so urgent to Him *that He sovereignly arranged the sun and the moon to perfectly align themselves to create a* Tetrad—*four consecutive blood moons.* (42)

- Reread Joel 2:31 and Acts 2:20. What two astronomical events are repeated in these verses?

Blood Moon

A "blood moon" is a total lunar eclipse in which the moon appears to be red in color. When the earth is perfectly aligned between the sun and the moon, the earth's shadow completely covers the moon, causing a total lunar eclipse. When this happens, the sun's rays pass through the earth's atmosphere and cast on the moon a red shadow, much like a sunset. Blood moons happen reasonably often. But Four Blood Moons that happen in sequence are an extreme rarity.

CHAPTER 3: WARNING COMES BEFORE JUDGMENT

The Bible clearly describes both blood moons and a solar eclipse in Joel 2:30–31 and Acts 2:19–20, and Jesus confirms them in Matthew 24:29 saying, "Immediately after the tribulation of those days the sun will be darkened and the moon will not give its light." (44)

- Look up the following astronomical terms online (or review them on pages 43–44 of *Four Blood Moons*) and write the definitions below:

   Lunar Eclipse:

   Blood Moon:

   Solar Eclipse:

   Tetrad:

God's "Set Time"—The Roman, Julian, Gregorian, and Jewish Calendars

God has an exact set time *for all things to happen.* (42)

• Read Habakkuk 2:2–4. What does this passage show us about God's timetable? Who sets the times for future events? How certain can we be that these appointed times will come and the prophetic events be fulfilled?

• When we look into God's exact "set time" for future events, we must keep in mind that our Western calendar is not the same as the Jewish calendar, on which biblical prophecies are based. Review the four main calendars described on pages 45–46 of *Four Blood Moons* and write a brief explanation of each in the space below:

    Roman Calendar:

    Julian Calendar:

    Gregorian Calendar:

    Jewish Calendar:

• Which calendar coordinates all three major astronomical phenomena—the rotation of the earth, the revolution of the moon around the earth, and the revolution of the earth around the sun?

- Why is it important to understand the differences between these calendars? What could happen if we tried to calculate God's timetable according to a calendar other than the one He outlined for His people in sacred Scripture?

Jewish Calendar Compared to Gregorian Calendar[2]

Month	Length	Gregorian Equivalent
Nissan	30 days	March–April
Iyar	29 days	April–May
Sivan	30 days	May–June
Tammuz	29 days	June–July
Av	30 days	July–August
Elul	29 days	August–September
Tishri	30 days	September–October
Heshvan	29 or 30 days	October–November
Kislev	30 or 29 days	November–December
Tevet	29 days	December–January
Shevat	30 days	January–February
Adar	29 or 30 days	February–March
Adar II (leap year)	29 days	March–April

Note: This is a general guideline for the corresponding Gregorian months in the Western civil calendar. Many websites provide exact Jewish-calendar-to-Western-calendar conversions for specific years.

A BOOK OF SEVENS

The Bible is a book of sevens.... God uses the number seven to measure time and judgments. (47, 49)

- Read Genesis 2:2–3. How many days are in a week, according to God's design? According to Exodus 16:26, what is the seventh day called?

- Read Leviticus 25:1–4. Just as God set aside every *seventh day* of the week as a *Sabbath day*, God designed every *seventh year* to be a *Sabbath year*. Write below what God commands His people to do during this Sabbath year—also called a *Shemittah* year.

- Read Leviticus 25:8–17. Every fiftieth year (the year after the seventh Sabbath year) is another special time set aside for God. According to v. 13, what is this fiftieth year to be called? What is supposed to happen during this year?

Shemittah

The Hebrew word *shemittah* comes from a root word meaning "letting go." It is translated in the Old Testament as "remission" or "release"— usually in reference to releasing someone from debt or from slavery. Because God commanded all debts to be forgiven every seventh year, the Sabbath year began to be called the "year of release," or *Shemittah* year. (See Deuteronomy 15:1, 9; 31:10.)[3]

THE SHEMITTAH YEAR

Shemittah is the Sabbatical year, which occurs every seventh year. Shemittah is "Shabbat" (the Sabbath) for the land of Israel; the land "rests" in a fashion, similar to the way the Jewish people rest every seventh day. (49)

- Read Leviticus 25:4–5. What were the Jewish people forbidden to do during the Shemittah year?

- God knew the people of Israel might worry about how they would survive during the Shemittah year and ask Him, "What shall we eat in the seventh year, since we shall not sow nor gather in our produce?" (v. 20). Write God's answer as stated in Leviticus 25:21–22.

- Read Jeremiah 34:12–22. What severe consequences did God impose when the people did not honor the Shemittah year?

- Why do you think the Shemittah year is so important to God? How does honoring the Shemittah year demonstrate complete trust in God's provision?

- Read 2 Chronicles 36:15–21. According to this passage, what was one reason God allowed the Jewish people to be exiled to Babylon? What did the land experience while the people were gone?

AMERICA UNDER JUDGMENT

In America the judgment of violating Shemittah is not linked to the land of Israel but to our national disobedience to the Word of God. (50)

- While observing the Shemittah guarantees abundance and blessing, neglecting it leads to judgment. Below are the most recent Shemittah years. (Note that Shemittah years are measured according to the Jewish calendar, in which the civil new year corresponds to the American month September.) Write beside each year a catastrophic event that occurred in America that could possibly correspond with the judgment of God on a nation that has neglected His Word:

    September 2001:

    September 2008:

- The next Shemittah year will begin on September 25, 2014, and end on September 13, 2015. What is significant about these dates in relation to the coming Four Blood Moons? Do you think the two events could be connected? Why or why not?

• QUESTIONS FOR GROUP DISCUSSION •

- Discuss the following statement: *If what God's Word says about the creation is not true, why would you believe His Word when He says, "Call to Me and I will answer you, and show you great and mighty things, which you do not know" (Jeremiah 33:3)? If*

Genesis 1:1 is not true, why bother believing in the remainder of God's Word? (31). Do you believe that Genesis 1:1 is true? Why or why not? How does this affect your view of the rest of the Bible?

- What insights did you learn about God's absolute control over the heavens in your study of biblical passages this week? Give specific examples. If your group has time, discuss what you learned this week while reading chapter 10 of this study guide: "Are There Other Biblical Prophecies Involving the Sun, Moon, and Stars?"

- What is the significance of the Shemittah year? What happens when a nation honors the Shemittah year? What happens when a nation neglects God's Word and dishonors the Shemittah year? Discuss the catastrophic events that affected America in September 2001 and September 2008. What possible consequences could befall our nation in 2014–15 if we continue to disobey God's Word?

PRAYER

Heavenly Father, we declare our absolute belief that You alone are the Creator of the heavens and the earth. You have total control of the sun, moon, and stars; and You have the power to direct them however You will. We are grateful that You have not left us without witness, but You have promised that You will announce the signs of Your coming in the heavens. We repent of all the years we have neglected Your Word and Your ways. Restore our lives and our nation,

Lord, as we seek to honor You from this time forth and forevermore. In the name of our Messiah, King Jesus, amen.

TAKE ACTION

- Commit to read and study the Scriptures on a regular basis so you are ready to walk in obedience and not neglect God's Word. If you want to join me in receiving a daily Scripture reading plan, I invite you to go to www.jhm.org and sign up for the Daily Scripture Reading and Pastoral Blessing.

- *Do you need direction for your life? Follow the star of Bethlehem; it will lead to Christ. Wise men looked for Him then and wise men still follow Him today (Matthew 2:9)* (38). Do you need direction for your life in a specific area? Do you want to know God's will for you and your loved ones? Turn to Jesus and seek Him above all else. Choose the way of wisdom by writing below the area(s) you are committing to Jesus today, and allow Him to work through you.

- Ask God to search your heart and reveal to you any ways you have been withholding from Him what is rightfully His. Are you honoring Him right now with your time, your talents, and your tithe? If not, write out specific action steps you can take to begin to honor God's Word and give back to Him out of the abundance He has given you.

WEEK 3:
End-Times Prophecy

⚜

STUDY OF CHAPTERS 4–5 IN *FOUR BLOOD MOONS*

....

Before we can fully grasp the significance of the coming
Four Blood Moons, we must know and understand the
spine of biblical prophecy concerning the end of the
world as we know it.

(*Four Blood Moons,* chapter 4)

....

Prepare for Week 3

- Read chapter 4, "The Spine of Prophecy," in *Four Blood Moons.*
- Read chapter 5, "When Will These Things Be?" in *Four Blood Moons.*

Key Verse

Now as He sat on the Mount of Olives, the disciples came to Him privately, saying, "Tell us, when will these things be? And what will be the sign of Your coming, and of the end of the age?"

—Matthew 24:3

Key Passage from *Four Blood Moons*

The Author of Matthew 24 is the only Master Teacher of Prophecy who ever lived—Jesus Christ, the Son of God, the Son of David, our King, and our Redeemer. Let's join Jesus, the Rabbi, and the twelve disciples at His Prophecy Conference on the Mount of Olives.

—*Four Blood Moons,* chapter 4

✧

• Questions for Personal Study •

Chapter 4: The Spine of Prophecy

In many ways the spine determines the health of the whole body. That's the reason I have titled this seminal chapter "The Spine of Prophecy." As long as each prophetic vertebra is in place, it produces peace and confidence concerning our future and the future of the world. Let one element (vertebra) of prophecy get distorted and you begin to suffer spiritually. Let more than one element get dislocated and your theology is skewed needing a scriptural adjustment to correct. (56)

- As we study end-times prophecy, why is it essential for each prophetic "vertebra" to be in place? What could happen if our understanding of prophecy becomes distorted?

- In what ways are the various prophecies in the Bible connected to each other? If we misinterpret one prophecy, how does that affect our overall understanding of coming events?

When discussing the signs of the times you want to find someone who is an absolute authority on Bible prophecy; someone who is always right and has never had to change his prophecy chart. Well, I have found that Someone. *He is the Living Word!* (51)

- Why is it important to base our interpretation of prophecy on an absolute expert? What is the danger of trusting someone other than an absolute authority when it comes to interpreting the signs of the times?

- How do we know Jesus Christ is the absolute authority on biblical prophecy? Read Matthew 11:27 and John 1:14. What do these verses tell us about Jesus' relationship to the Father—and, as a result, His understanding of what God will do in the future?

THE PROPHECY CONFERENCE

The disciples gather closely; this is the moment Jesus has chosen to share the future with them—the very Spine of Prophecy. (57)

- Read Matthew 19:28–29. What do you think the disciples were expecting to happen? What did they think Jesus was going to do? How do you think they envisioned their future with Him?

- Read Zechariah 14:4 and compare it to Matthew 24:3. How would Jesus' choice of location for His Prophecy Conference have heightened the disciples' expectation about being an important part of a coming kingdom?

SATAN'S SNARE

America is going the wrong way, and in our vainglorious pride we have refused to change direction. (60)

- Read Proverbs 16:18. According to this verse, what attitude precedes destruction? Why?

- In what ways do you see evidence of pride in your own life? Be specific. List them below. (Writing them out might be a painful process, but it is an act of confession that will free you from the burden of sin.) Now repent before God of each of them, crossing them off your list as you receive God's abundant cleansing and forgiveness (1 John 1:9).

- In what ways do you see evidence of the sin of pride in the current actions and attitudes of our nation? Explain your answers.

THE ROMANS' DESTRUCTION OF THE TEMPLE

As the disciples gazed at this massive structure, they found Jesus' words about its destruction impossible to believe. (62)

The Jewish Temple in the Time of Jesus

Herod the Great had a passion for buildings. In the eighteenth year of his reign, Herod ordered that the Jewish Temple be rebuilt in a magnificent scale. He enlarged the Temple area to approximately thirty-five acres. The massive building project took forty-six years to complete. (See John 2:20.)[1]

- Read Matthew 24:2. Considering the massive scale and splendor of the Temple that stood in Jerusalem during the time of Christ, how do you think the disciples responded when they heard this prophecy? How would you have responded?

- In what ways did Jesus' foreboding words of the coming destruction of the Temple contradict what the disciples expected?

Exactly as Jesus had prophesied, the Temple was destroyed when the Romans seized Jerusalem just four years after it was completed . . . on the 9th of Av, a date that proved over and over to be infamous in the history of the Jewish people. (62)

The 9th of Av

The 9th of Av (*Tisha B'Av*) is an annual day of fasting for the Jews. On this day of mourning, Jews remember the many national tragedies that occurred on the 9th of Av, such as the destruction of the First and Second Temples, the First Crusade, the Jewish expulsion from England, and the Spanish Inquisition. The 9th of Av is considered by many to be the saddest day in the Jewish calendar.

CHAPTER 5: WHEN WILL THESE THINGS BE?

The twelve disciples are now getting the picture—Jesus is going to be killed. . . . the Temple would be destroyed, and the nation of Israel scattered. So what was to come? (65)

- Reread Matthew 24:3. List below the three questions the disciples asked Jesus:

  1.

  2.

  3.

- What specific event do you think the "end of the age" refers to? What is the difference between the "end of the age" and the Rapture of the church? (We will learn more about the Rapture in week 4.)

ROMAN DESTRUCTION OF JERUSALEM

Jesus looked into the bewildered faces of His disciples and warned

them that in the immediate future an invading army would sur-
round and destroy the sacred city of Jerusalem. (67)

- Look up the word *desolation* in a dictionary and write out the definition below. What strikes you about this definition in relation to the splendor of the sacred city of Jerusalem?

- Read Matthew 24:15–16 and compare it to Daniel 9:27. How do you think the disciples responded when Jesus described their beloved city—the thriving home of the Temple and focal point of God's people—in these horrific terms? (You will learn more about the "abomination of desolation" in week 6.)

- Turn to pages 68–70 of *Four Blood Moons* and read through the atrocities that occurred during the Roman army's siege of Jerusalem in AD 70, as recorded by the historian Josephus. Jot down in the space below a few of the incidents that occurred during this time. This destruction of Jerusalem fulfilled the first part of Jesus' Prophecy Conference.

JERUSALEM—THE CITY OF GOD

Jerusalem is not like any other city on earth; the world revolves around Jerusalem. Jerusalem is the city of God! (71)

- Read the following verses and write out what God says about His city, Jerusalem:

Psalm 132:13:

Psalm 48:1–2, 8:

- What does Psalm 137:5–6 tell us about the importance of the city of Jerusalem? What should be our attitude toward this city?

- List a few of the significant historical events associated with the city of Jerusalem. (If you need hints, see pages 71–73 of *Four Blood Moons*.)

- Read Zechariah 14:16–18 and Isaiah 24:23. According to these passages, what significant future event will take place in Jerusalem? Describe it below.

For more information on Jerusalem and its role in world history and God's plan, turn to part 2 of this study guide and read chapter 11: "Why Is Jerusalem Significant to God's Plan?"

Jerusalem will remain the center of the universe for the future of the world! (74)

• QUESTIONS FOR GROUP DISCUSSION •

- Have you, like the twelve disciples, ever expected Jesus to be or do something—only to have Him reveal to you that His plan is completely different than what you imagined it would be? Discuss your experiences. Talk about how you would feel if you were one of Jesus' twelve disciples asking Him questions on the

Mount of Olives that day. What would you be hoping? How do you think you would respond? How would Jesus' answer affect your faith and your future?

- What is the difference between "the end of the age" and the Rapture? Discuss any insights you may have learned in your study this week. To which of these two events does Jesus refer in the Olivet Discourse (Matthew 24)? Do the "signs" of the solar and lunar eclipses in this passage point to the Rapture of the church or to some other significant future event? Why? Support your answers with Scripture.

- Discuss what you learned this week about the significance of the city of Jerusalem in world history. What historical events happened there? What future historical event will happen there? Why is Jerusalem such an important city? Support your answers with the Bible. If your group has time, discuss the insights you learned this week by reading chapter 11 of this study guide: "Why Is Jerusalem Significant to God's Plan?"

Prayer

Heavenly Father, thank You for giving us the Absolute Expert in biblical prophecy in Your Son, Jesus Christ. Help us always to seek His words and His wisdom whenever considering the events of the future. Thank You for giving us a glimpse of Your plan for Your Holy City, Jerusalem, this week. Whenever we are tempted to fear what our future might hold, give us assurance and Your peace, which passes all understanding. Remind us that You are the Author of all history—past, present, and future—and Your plan for us is good and perfect. In Jesus' name we pray, amen.

TAKE ACTION

- *Pride is a cancer that kills everything and everyone it touches. Is it in your church? Is it in your family? Is it in you? Get it out now! Your very spiritual survival is at stake* (61). Look over your answers in the "Satan's Snare" section. Is there any root of pride in your life that you have not confessed? If so, confess and repent of it now!

- Look up current news headlines about events taking place in the city of Jerusalem today. Have your attitudes about these stories changed as a result of your study this week? Go to your Internet browser and bookmark news sites such the *Jerusalem Post* (www.jpost.com) to stay up-to-date on current events in Jerusalem and the nation of Israel. Note: do not rely solely on American media outlets for the full story.

- When you consider your future—especially in light of end-times biblical prophecy—are you tempted to fear what lies ahead for you? If so, confess your fear to God. Name your fear by writing it in the space below. Then say the following verse out loud: "When I am afraid, I will put my trust in You. In God, whose word I praise, in God I have put my trust; I shall not be afraid" (Psalm 56:3–4 NASB). Now cross out the fear you wrote below as you say a prayer of thanksgiving to God for replacing your fear with faith.

WEEK 4:

The Rapture and Israel

⚜

STUDY OF CHAPTERS 6–7 IN *FOUR BLOOD MOONS*

....

The fact that men do not believe Christ is coming back
is living proof and biblical evidence that the Rapture
of the church is imminent. If you listen closely you
can hear the footsteps of Messiah . . .
tiptoeing through the clouds of heaven.

(*Four Blood Moons*, chapter 6)

....

Prepare for Week 4

- Read chapter 6, "Concerning the Rapture," in *Four Blood Moons*.
- Read chapter 7, "Land of Promise, Land of Pain," in *Four Blood Moons*.

KEY VERSE

The Lord Himself will descend from heaven with a shout,
with the voice of an archangel, and with the trumpet of God.
And the dead in Christ will rise first. Then we who are alive
and remain shall be caught up together with them *in the
clouds* to meet the Lord in the air.

—1 THESSALONIANS 4:16–17

KEY PASSAGE FROM *FOUR BLOOD MOONS*

*When the time comes, the trumpet of God shall sound, announcing
the appearance of royalty, for He is the Prince of Peace, the King of
kings and the Lord of lords. He is coming in the clouds of heaven
for those who are watching for His glorious appearing. Look up, my
friends, for the King is coming!*

—*Four Blood Moons*, chapter 6

• QUESTIONS FOR PERSONAL STUDY •

CHAPTER 6: CONCERNING THE RAPTURE

America is filled with false prophets. . . . Some of these false prophets are now teaching there will be no Rapture of the church! What does God's Word say? Why is it extremely important for you to know the truth about this doctrine? (78)

* The apostle Paul clearly taught the doctrine of the Rapture of the church. Read 1 Thessalonians 4:16–17 and write out below the specific events that will happen during the Rapture:

Rapture

The word Rapture is taken from the Latin translation of "caught up" in 1 Thessalonians 4:17. I believe this verse, along with many others throughout the Bible, teaches that Jesus Christ will come for His church in an event called the Rapture, which will occur before the seven years of the Great Tribulation, led by the Antichrist. The Rapture, which happens before the Great Tribulation, is separate from Jesus' Second Coming, which occurs at the end of the seven-year tribulation. Many people ask me what signs must be fulfilled before the church will be raptured from the earth. The answer is *zero!* Not one thing needs to happen before the Rapture can occur. The Rapture of the church is imminent; it could happen before you finish reading this page. Get ready! The King is coming!

- Read 1 Corinthians 15:51–52. How do these verses relate to the event described in 1 Thessalonians 4:16–17? What additional insights do these verses reveal about the Rapture?

- What does Acts 1:11 reveal about the Rapture? What will it look like?

THE TRUTH—THE RAPTURE IS COMING

The point is very clear: . . . If you're not watching for Him, *He's not coming for* you! (78–79)

- What does Jesus command His followers to do in Luke 21:36?

- Read Hebrews 9:28. To whom will Jesus appear a second time?

- Are you "eagerly waiting" for Jesus to Rapture you, along with His church? If not, will you commit to doing so right now? Write out your commitment below.

- What would eager anticipation of the Rapture look like in your everyday life? Take a moment to imagine how this outlook—*The Rapture could happen at any moment!*—could affect all areas of your life. Write some of your thoughts below:

  how you spend your time:

  how your spend your money:

  how you relate to other people:

The Real Jesus

If you don't believe in the Rapture as described in the Bible, where believers rise to meet the Lord in the air, how will you know when the real Jesus comes to earth? (81)

- Read Matthew 24:23–24. What does Jesus say will happen before His Second Coming? How should His followers respond?

Satan hates the Rapture teaching and has his deluded disciples saying there will be no Rapture. (83)

- What does the apostle Peter say about these false teachers in 2 Peter 2:1? What will happen to these false teachers?

- How will we know when the real Jesus gets here?

Stay on the Alert

Jesus Christ is telling us to stay on the alert *and to* wake up! *Because if we are not watching for His return, we will miss His coming and will not escape the future horrors of the Antichrist, and we will not receive the crown of life.* (87)

- Read Luke 21:36 and Revelation 3:3. What attitude does Jesus expect us to have toward the coming Rapture of the church?

- Reread the depictions of the Rapture on pages 88–89 of *Four Blood Moons.* What images stand out to you? What other consequences could the sudden disappearance of millions of Christians have on our world? What effects would the Rapture have on your community . . . your workplace . . . your own family?

We are commanded to "watch," which means we must know the Spine of Prophecy and diligently look for God's announcements in the heavens through signs such as the Four Blood Moons. The Bible is clear that only those who "watch" will be counted worthy to escape those things that are coming on the earth. (91)

HAS THE RAPTURE HAPPENED?

The deception that Jesus warned us about in Matthew 24 is spreading in our generation like a contagious theological virus with lies such as Jesus has already returned and the rapture of the church is a thing of the past. Not so! (94)

- The Bible is clear that the Rapture will occur *before* the seven-year Great Tribulation. The Tribulation begins in Revelation 6, with the arrival of the Four Horsemen of the Apocalypse. Turn in your Bible to the book of Revelation and briefly skim through the events of the Great Tribulation, described in Revelation chapters 6, 8, and 9. Have any of those events occurred yet? If not, what does that tell you about whether the Rapture has occurred yet?

- Read 2 Thessalonians 2:1–5. What specific events does the apostle Paul say have to happen *before* "the day of the Lord"?

Make a list of them. As you do, remember, that "the day of the Lord" refers to the day of God's judgment on the earth that occurs *after* the Rapture and *after* the Great Tribulation.

- Based on what you have learned from the Bible so far, list the following events in chronological order below: *Great Tribulation, Rapture, Day of the Lord.*

  1.

  2.

  3.

- Now reread Joel 2:30–31 and write out any new insights you have learned this week about the Blood Moons. When will they appear? Are these Blood Moons a sign of the coming of the *Rapture* or a sign of the coming of "the day of the Lord"? What affect does this understanding have on your view of the coming Four Blood Moons?

Chapter 7: Land of Promise, Land of Pain
No piece of real estate on planet earth has been more contested than the land of Israel even though God clearly gave it to the Jewish people forever. (99)

- Read Genesis 17:18–21. Based on these verses, to whom does the land belong? How would you respond to someone who claims the land of Israel belongs to the descendants of Ishmael? Are the descendants of Ishmael (modern-day Palestinians) included in the biblical mandate to own the land?

- Read Galatians 4:21–31. In what ways does the apostle Paul, in the New Testament, confirm the Old Testament reality that the geographic land of Israel belongs to the descendants of Isaac, not the descendants of Ishmael?

The greatest geopolitical threat to America and the world can be resolved by answering the question: to whom does the land of Israel truly belong? God resolved this controversy centuries ago. (102)

- Take a few minutes to read through the twenty-five Scripture passages listed on pages 102–10 in *Four Blood Moons*. Underline the passages that are significant to you. Circle the words *forever, everlasting,* and *covenant.* Write below what you learn about the land of Israel from these verses.

- Read Numbers 34:10–15 and Deuteronomy 32:8–10. What do these verses tell you about the borders of the land of Israel? Who set the borders?

- Read Joel 3:2. What does God say He will do to the nations who try to drive out the descendants of Isaac from their rightful, God-given land of Israel?

For further study on the role of Israel in God's plan, turn to part 2 of this study guide and read chapter 12: "Why Should Christians Support Israel?"

THE DECEIT OF REPLACEMENT THEOLOGY

Replacement Theology is intellectually and scripturally dishonest. I believe Replacement Theology is religious anti-Semitism; it is one of the most dangerous forms of deception in the church today. (118)

Replacement Theology

Replacement Theology, also called *Supersessionism*, is a doctrine that holds to three false concepts:

1. God is finished with the Jewish people.
2. The Christian church is the "New Israel" and takes the place of the Jewish people forever.
3. God has broken His covenant with the Jewish people and has replaced it with His covenant with the church.

- Why is the false doctrine of Replacement Theology so dangerous for the Christian church today? How can this doctrine affect our attitude toward Israel and the Jewish people?

- Read Numbers 23:19, Hebrews 6:18, and Titus 1:2. Based on these verses, write your answer to this question: *Can God lie?*

- If God cannot lie, then can He break His promises to the Jewish people—including all twenty-five promises listed earlier in this chapter?

- Has God "cast away" His people and replaced them with the church? Read Romans 11:1, 11. How does Paul respond to that question? What insights does the apostle Paul give us about

God's current relationship to the Jewish people?

God has not replaced Israel, because as we will see in coming chapters, His heavenly billboard of the Four Blood Moons is directly tied to significant events in the history of the Jewish people. (115)

• QUESTIONS FOR GROUP DISCUSSION •

- What did you learn this week about the Rapture of the church? How is the Rapture different than the Second Coming of Christ? Which event occurs first? According to the Bible, what will the Rapture look like? Who will be raptured? How will it happen? What prophetic signs have to be fulfilled before the Rapture can take place?

- Why do you think Satan hates the doctrine of the Rapture and tries so hard to spread deception in the church about this event? Discuss this statement: *The rapture is Christ's celebration over death, hell, and the grave which He defeated when He died on the cross. It is the ultimate humiliation of Satan* (83).

- What did you learn in your study this week about Replacement Theology? What does this doctrine teach? How would you respond, based on the Bible, to someone who believes this doctrine? Does the truth of God's continued covenant with Israel in any way diminish or take away from His covenant with the church? Explain. Remember, *Israel and the church are unique. The church never replaces Israel, and Israel never replaces the church* (118). If you have time, discuss any insights you learned from reading chapter 12 of this study guide: "Why Should Christians Support Israel?"

PRAYER

Heavenly Father, we know that we will either bow before the Antichrist or bow before Jesus Christ. It is not a question of if we will bow; it's only a matter of when we will bow. We choose to bow today before our Lord and Savior, Jesus Christ. He is the Son of God, the coming Messiah, the King of kings, the One to whom all praise is due. We choose to live today—and every day—in eager anticipation of His imminent Rapture of the church, where He will catch us up in the clouds, together with all believers, and bring us into His glorious presence forever. In the name of our one and only Savior and Redeemer we pray, amen.

TAKE ACTION

- Imagine your doctor telling you that you only have twenty-four hours to live. What would you do? What would you say? In what ways would you live differently? Jot in the margin a few things you would do if you knew tomorrow was your last day on earth. Now apply that attitude to the reality that the Rapture is imminent—it could happen at any moment, even before you finish this lesson! Look over your list of what you would do on your last day on earth—and make any changes in your life based on this reality.

- Read aloud the list of biblical truths on pages 84–85 of *Four Blood Moons*. If you are in a group, take turns proclaiming the literal truths revealed to us in Scripture. Thank God for His literal, absolute, clear, and perfect Truth!

• Share your confidence with others this week, telling them why you can walk in assurance in face of global uncertainty and fear. Write letters or send e-mails to your unbelieving friends and loved ones, proclaiming God's truth and the gospel so that even after you are "caught up" with Jesus in the Rapture, they can refer back to your words and come to faith.

The Beginning of the End?

⚶

Study of Chapters 8–9 in *Four Blood Moons*

We can see the storm gathering in the Middle East and, again, Israel is the key. . . . God is watching! The final drama is unfolding before our eyes as you read it on the front pages of your newspaper and watch it on the national news almost every night.

(*Four Blood Moons*, chapter 8)

Prepare for Week 5

- Read chapter 8, "Wars and Rumors of Wars," in *Four Blood Moons*.
- Read chapter 9, "Famine, Earthquakes, and Anarchy," in *Four Blood Moons*.

KEY VERSE

You will hear of wars and rumors of wars, but see to it that you are not alarmed. Such things must happen, but the end is still to come. Nation will rise against nation, and kingdom against kingdom.

—MATTHEW 24:6–7 NIV1984

KEY PASSAGE FROM *FOUR BLOOD MOONS*

God Almighty created the Jewish State and has sworn to defend it. Anyone—politicians from Haman to Hitler, military giants from Goliath to Iran, or any tormentor from Pharaoh to Putin—that presents an existential threat to Israel will utterly be destroyed by the hand of the Lord.

—*Four Blood Moons*, chapter 8

⚓

• QUESTIONS FOR PERSONAL STUDY •

CHAPTER 8: WARS AND RUMORS OF WARS

Jesus told us that before His second coming, we "will hear of wars and rumors of wars" and that "nation will rise against nation, and kingdom against kingdom" (Matthew 24:6–7 NIV1984). I believe that "nation will rise against nation" describes all major physical wars on earth from the time of Christ until today, including the wars against Israel. (121)

- Read Genesis 17:7–8. What does God do in these verses? What specific land does He give to the descendants of Abraham? How long will the land belong to them?

- Read Psalm 121:2–4. According to this passage, who watches over Israel? Does He ever take a break from defending His people?

"Keeping" Israel

The word translated "keeps" or "watches over" in Psalm 121:4 is the Hebrew word *shamar*, which means "to protect, guard, preserve." Other translations of this verse call God the "Protector of Israel" or "Guardian of Israel." The picture is of a military guard or sentinel who is alert, equipped, and ready to defend his charge against any threat or attack.

- What happened to the enemies of Israel when they tried to annihilate the Jewish people as they journeyed from Egypt to the Promised Land? Read Joshua 10:10–11 to find out.

- Read page 121 in *Four Blood Moons* to find out two other Old Testament biblical characters who rose up against the nation of Israel—only to suffer defeat at the hands of the God who "keeps Israel" (Psalm 121:4). In the space below, write out their

names, what they tried to do to the Jewish people, and how
God defeated them:

1.

2.

KINGDOM SHALL RISE AGAINST KINGDOM

*I believe Jesus' prophecy that kingdom shall rise against kingdom
(Matthew 24:7) is a description of the kingdom of light versus the
kingdom of darkness.* (127)

- What evidence can we see of the battle between good and evil
  in our society today? Consider current programming on television, movies, books, and the Internet. In what ways have the
  occult, witchcraft, sorcery, and demonic elements subtly wo-
  ven themselves into popular culture and entertainment? Give
  specific examples.

- How is the battle between good and evil demonstrating itself in our schools? What are some of the things our children
  are being taught in public schools and universities—and how
  does that teaching compare to the truth of the Word of God?

For more information about whether the Four Blood Moons could be connected to end-times
events, turn to part 2 of this study guide and read chapter 13: "How Do the Four Blood Moons
Relate to the Gog-Magog War?"

CHAPTER 9: FAMINE, EARTHQUAKES, AND ANARCHY
The world, including *America, is inching toward a time when we will no longer be able to produce the food it takes to feed our people.* (132–33)

• Read Revelation 6:5–6. These verses describe a global famine that will occur during the Great Tribulation. (Note: according to Matthew 20:2, a "denarius" represents one day's wages.) Although the church will have already been raptured at this point in history, what will this famine be like for those who remain on the earth during that time?

• How would extreme famine affect every other part of life? What would people be willing to do for food? What possible consequences could arise as a result of this global famine?

• In what ways does the decline of the American family farm contribute to our vulnerability to this kind of famine? Does our nation have sufficient land and crops to feed our population if outside supplies were suddenly cut off? How do our nation's current policies of the death tax and foreign subsidies contribute to food shortages?

THERE WILL BE PESTILENCES
Nothing can stop a plague once it starts. . . . The strong will survive, and the weak will die. (135)

• Read Revelation 6:7–8, which describes a time of global disease and death. How many people will die as a result of the sword, famine, and plague?

- Consider how our current technology and international connectedness could contribute to a global plague. Diseases that used to take weeks, even months, to cross the ocean can now infect people across the globe within hours on an international flight. Write down some recent examples of diseases (such as the swine flu, H1N1, SARS, bird flu, etc.) that raced across the globe and caused a worldwide scare within days.

THERE WILL BE EARTHQUAKES

God uses earthquakes to get the attention of those who are spiritually hard of hearing. (137)

- Read Acts 16:25–28. How did God use an earthquake to shake up His followers and bring people to salvation?

- By what means does God protect Jerusalem from enemies, according to Isaiah 29:6?

- Revelation 16:18–20 describes the greatest earthquake in all of human history, which will occur during the Great Tribulation. Write below the catastrophic effects of that earthquake.

THE UNITED STATES OF ANARCHY

America has a lack of leadership within our government, and we are seeing anarchy on a national level never seen in our history. (140)

Anarchy

Anarchy is defined by *Merriam-Webster* as "a state of lawlessness or political disorder due to the absence of governmental authority." When authority goes out, anarchy comes in. Our nation has abandoned God's holy laws in favor of political correctness. We are seeing a rise in anarchy today as the church watches our nation's moral free fall in silence and will not take a stand on tough issues. Today the church has ordained lifestyles that God calls an abomination. We have thrown out the Ten Commandments, and our government condones the practices of witchcraft and Satanism. We cover the stench of sin with tolerance and prioritize being all-inclusive instead of demanding adherence to the Word of God![1]

- In His Prophecy Conference, Jesus told His disciples that in the last days before His Second Coming, "lawlessness will abound" (Matthew 24:12). Describe some current, specific examples of "lawlessness" abounding in our society today.

- Read 2 Thessalonians 2:8–11. What title is used for the Antichrist in this passage?

- In what ways is the current attitude of our nation much like the description of the people of Israel in Judges 21:25?

- What happens when discipline and order are removed from a nation's government, schools, and homes? Write out a few specific examples of current events that demonstrate the result of people who have no respect for law, authority, or discipline in our society.

- Read Psalm 9:17. What will happen to those nations who turn away from God?

- In contrast to a nation where lawlessness and anarchy abound, how does Psalm 33:12 describe a nation that follows God?

• QUESTIONS FOR GROUP DISCUSSION •

- As you did your study this week, how did you feel when you realized that wars, famines, pestilences, and earthquakes are occurring more and more often in recent years? Do you see any connection between current events and the signs of the coming of the day of the Lord that Jesus told His disciples about in Matthew 24? What could that mean for our current generation? What "signs of the times" can we currently observe in our own world? If you have time, discuss what you learned from reading chapter 13 of this study guide: "How Do the Four Blood Moons Relate to the Gog-Magog War?"

- What evidences of lawlessness and anarchy are you seeing in our nation today? Describe a time you rebelled against authority or were the victim of someone else's lawlessness. What was your experience like? How did you feel? What were the consequences?

- Read Psalm 33:12 aloud. Describe what "a nation whose God is the LORD" would look like. What would its politics be? How

65

would its economy operate? Discuss whether you think it is possible for America to become that kind of nation once again. What role(s) could you play in our nation's repentance and restoration?

PRAYER

Heavenly Father, Your Word is truth. Please open our eyes and hearts to the truth of Your Word that we may know You and that we may not be deceived by false theology. Examine our hearts and show us ways we can prepare to be ready to meet You. Help us to walk confidently in obedience to Your Word and the law of the land—as long as the law of the land not does force us to deny You. Help us always to obey You and Your Word so that when You come, You will find faith on the earth. Amen.

TAKE ACTION

- *If America is to survive, there must be a time of national repentance for our sins and a return to the eternal truths of the Word of God* (129). Gather one or two friends and set up a prayer group to fast and pray regularly for our nation. Jesus promises us, "Where two or three are gathered together in My name, I am there in the midst of them" (Matthew 18:20).

- Commit to memorize at least one verse a week so you will hide God's Word in your heart and walk in a manner worthy of Him. When you have passages of Scripture committed to memory, you will be prepared not only for daily life, but also prepared to be faithful during future persecution of the church. People can take away your Bible, but they cannot take away the Word you have stored in your heart.

- Take action in our nation! Keep up with current events, and get involved—sending e-mails or phone calls to representatives and senators, attending local political meetings, and making sure you vote! Take steps to help others be alert and informed about the events in our nation and around our world.

WEEK 6:

The Tribulation and Second Coming

⚘

STUDY OF CHAPTERS 10–11 IN *FOUR BLOOD MOONS*

Without a clear and concise understanding of
God's plan, which is revealed in Scripture, then the Four
Blood Moons would be nothing more than a spectacular
cosmic occurrence as opposed to the fulfillment of
prophecy. There is a reason God has alerted us to
"look up" for the coming of the Lord.
His return is closer than you think.
(*Four Blood Moons*, chapter 11)

Prepare for Week 6

- Read chapter 10, "The Gospel of the Kingdom," in *Four Blood Moons*.
- Read chapter 11, "The Second Coming," in *Four Blood Moons*.

KEY VERSE

Then the sign of the Son of Man will appear in heaven,
and then all the tribes of the earth will mourn,
and they will see the Son of Man coming on the clouds
of heaven with great power and glory.

—MATTHEW 24:30

KEY PASSAGE FROM *FOUR BLOOD MOONS*

God created the earth, and as the Owner of planet earth He made a divine covenant with Abraham, Isaac, and Jacob that the land of Israel was theirs forever. From the book of Genesis until this day, tyrants and dictators have done everything in their power to take the land of Israel away from the Jewish people.

The day is soon coming when God Almighty is going to crush the enemies of Israel once and for all.

—*Four Blood Moons*, chapter 11

⚹

• QUESTIONS FOR PERSONAL STUDY •

CHAPTER 10: THE GOSPEL OF THE KINGDOM

During the reign of the Antichrist, the gospel of the kingdom *will be preached all over the world.* (146)

Gospel of the Kingdom

The gospel of salvation is the message of the first coming of Christ. This gospel speaks of Jesus' virgin birth, sinless life, death, and resurrection. The preaching of the gospel of salvation results in our redemption by grace through faith in Jesus Christ, which promises eternal life. This is the gospel the church is to preach until the time of the Rapture. After the Rapture, God will send messengers to preach *the gospel of the kingdom*, which is the message of the Second Coming of Christ. This gospel proclaims to the Jews and to the nations of the world, "Messiah is coming!"

• Read Matthew 24:14 and answer the questions below:

What will be preached?

To what extent will it be preached?

Why will it be preached?

What will happen *after* it has been preached?

- After the Rapture, God will send various messengers to preach the "gospel of the kingdom"—the message that Jesus, the Messiah, will return to earth in power and glory to judge the nations and rule over the earth from His throne in Jerusalem. Read Malachi 4:5; Revelation 11:3; and Revelation 14:6–7 to discover some of the ways God will communicate the gospel of the kingdom with the people on earth during the Great Tribulation.

- Read Romans 11:25–27. After the "fullness" (or "full number," NIV) of the Gentiles have been redeemed by the gospel of salvation, what will happen to the Jews left on earth at the time of Jesus' Second Coming?

Jesus now reminds His disciples of the coming perilous times referred to by the prophet Daniel as the "abomination of desolation." (148)

Abomination of Desolation

"Abomination of desolation" is a term used in the Bible to describe an action, usually made by a pagan leader, that is so heinous it desecrates (or makes unclean) the Temple in Jerusalem and results in the termination of the Jews' blood sacrifices there for the atonement of sin.

THE ABOMINATION OF ANTIOCHUS EPIPHANES
Daniel (7–6 BC) prophesied about the vicious Greek king Antiochus Epiphanes. (149)

- Read Daniel's prophecy of the "abomination of desolation" in Daniel 9:27 and Daniel 11:31. How does the prophet Daniel describe this future event and its connection to the Temple and blood sacrifices? Why would this event be so traumatic to the Jewish people?

Daniel was prophesying of the abomination of Antiochus Epiphanes, a Greek ruler who hated the Jewish people. In 167 BC, Antiochus defiled the Temple by sacrificing a pig (an unclean animal) on the altar and then erecting a statue of the Greek god Zeus to be worshipped in the Temple. Similar "abominations of desolation" were committed by the Roman general Titus in AD 70 and by the Roman emperor Hadrian in AD 117 (described in detail on pages 150–53 of *Four Blood Moons*). But by far, the most atrocious and evil "abomination of desolation" is yet to come—and it will happen at the hands of the Antichrist during the halfway mark of the seven-year tribulation period.

THE ABOMINATION OF THE ANTICHRIST

How will Israel and the Jewish people be able to finally identify the Antichrist? They will know by the specific sign that he will repeat the "abomination of desolation" of Antiochus Epiphanes, Titus, and Hadrian. (154–55)

- Read Matthew 24:15–20. In these verses, Jesus describes the future "abomination of desolation" by the Antichrist. Based on the descriptions given in Daniel's prophecies, what will happen to the Temple and to blood sacrifices at the time of the

Antichrist's abomination of desolation? According to Jesus, how should the Jews respond?

This coming Antichrist will be the ultimate "abomination of desolation" because he will introduce himself as god (Daniel 11:36–37; Revelation 13:5) and demand that the world worship him. He will set up his image in Jerusalem and present himself as the savior of the world. (154)

- Read Matthew 24:21. What event will occur immediately following the Antichrist's "abomination of desolation"?

- How does the prophet Daniel refer to the Great Tribulation in Daniel 12:1?

- Read the following verses and note the suffering that will take place during the Great Tribulation:

    Revelation 8:7
    Revelation 8:8–9
    Revelation 8:10–11
    Revelation 8:12
    Revelation 9:5–6
    Revelation 9:15

This kind of human suffering and massive death toll is beyond the mind of man to fathom and why Jesus Christ, the Son of God, accurately calls it the "great tribulation." (157)

LIGHTNING FROM THE EAST

When Jesus returns, He will illuminate the heavens. (158)

- Read Matthew 24:27. To what atmospheric phenomenon does Jesus compare His Second Coming? (Note: from what direction will He come?)

- Revelation 19:11–16 describes the Second Coming in greater detail. What do you learn from these verses about Jesus' return? What will He look like? Who is with Him?

Having told His disciples of the Great Tribulation (Matthew 24:15–29), the Rabbi continues His Olivet Discourse by describing the next major event in this prophetic digest of tomorrow's world. (161)

CHAPTER 11: THE SECOND COMING

Jesus Christ is coming back the second time to a world living in the unspeakable terror of the Great Tribulation. (163)

- How does Jesus describe the people's desperate search in Matthew 24:23–26? What are they looking for? What is Jesus' strong warning to His followers regarding these reports?

- What effect will Jesus' return have on all the tribes of the earth, according to Matthew 24:30? Why?

For more information on the events surrounding the return of Jesus Christ, turn to part 2 of this study guide and read chapter 14: "Will the Second Coming Happen in Our Lifetime?"

POWER AND GLORY

Jesus said that He will return "on the clouds of heaven with power and great glory" (Matthew 24:30). (164)

- Read the descriptions of Christ's first coming and Second Coming on page 165 of *Four Blood Moons*. Then chart below a few of the contrasts you observed:

JESUS' FIRST COMING	JESUS' SECOND COMING

GATHERING THE ELECT

The day is soon coming when God Almighty is going to crush the enemies of Israel once and for all. (166)

The Elect

"The elect" is a biblical term used in the Old Testament to refer to Israel, the nation that God has chosen. (See Isaiah 42:1; 45:4; 65:9.) In the New Testament, the term "elect" is broadened to include the church also. (See 2 Timothy 2:10; Titus 1:1.) But it is important to remember that in the Olivet Discourse, Jesus is discussing events that will take place *after* the church leaves earth in the Rapture. So all references to "the elect" in the Olivet Discourse (Matthew 24, Mark 13, Luke 21) refer to the Jewish people—not the church.

- Read Exodus 19:5–6. How does God describe the Jewish people (or "children of Israel") in these verses?

- What will the Son of Man do for His elect (the Jewish people) in Matthew 24:31?

- After Jesus gathers the elect, He will begin His millennial reign, during which the righteous Gentiles and Jewish people rule with the Messiah. Look up Isaiah 2:4 and Isaiah 11:6. How does the prophet Isaiah describe this golden age of peace?

• QUESTIONS FOR GROUP DISCUSSION •

- Discuss the differences between Jesus' first coming and His Second Coming that you studied under the "Power and Glory" section.

- What is the difference between the *gospel of salvation* and *the gospel of the kingdom*? Which one are we to be preaching today? Which one will be preached during the Great Tribulation? How do these two aspects of the gospel complement one another?

- Read Matthew 24:14 and discuss what will happen after the gospel of the kingdom is preached to the whole world. Think of ways the gospel can now reach all nations and peoples of the world much faster and easier with recent technological breakthroughs. As you consider current events alongside biblical prophecy, do you think we are getting close to the "end of the age"? Do you think it's possible that we might be the final generation on earth before Jesus raptures the church and the Great Tribulation begins? If you have time, discuss any insights you learned this week by reading chapter 14 of this study guide: "Will the Second Coming Happen in Our Lifetime?"

PRAYER

Heavenly Father, our hearts tremble when we hear of the turmoil and judgment to come. Give us a heart filled with Your peace, knowing that You are sovereignly in control of all things. We plead for a movement of the Holy Spirit over this nation to bring repentance and revival, starting with the house of the Lord . . . beginning with us. We pray for everyone we come in contact with, including our family, that we will be bold to share the gospel with them and live in such a way that will cause others to seek You.

TAKE ACTION

• The Bible urges us, "Examine yourselves as to whether you are in the faith" (2 Corinthians 13:5). Take a few moments to examine yourself and your heart. Have you accepted Jesus Christ as your Savior? Do you have the full assurance that you will be raptured, along with all other living Christians, when Jesus comes for His church? If not, then repent now and turn to Jesus for your salvation. For more information about how to be saved, see "Are You Ready?" at the end of this book.

• Though today's Christians will not be on earth during the Great Tribulation, many people will. Allow your heart to be grieved today for those who are deceived and lost. Pray for those you know by name. Let your knowledge of these future events give you an urgency to reach out to a lost world.

• Each generation is just one generation away from complete paganism. Don't let that generation begin with you! Set a plan to live a purposeful life in teaching and leading your family to know God and walk in obedience. As a family, discuss the situation in the world affecting Israel. Prepare to leave a legacy of faith for your children and loved ones.

WEEK 7:

The Four Blood Moons of 1493–94 and 1949–50

⚜

STUDY OF CHAPTERS 12–14 IN *FOUR BLOOD MOONS*

....

The world has taken a wrong turn and we need
a sign from God to get back on the right track—
the Four Blood Moons just may be that signal!
(*Four Blood Moons*, chapter 12)

....

Prepare for Week 7

- Read chapter 12, "The Four Blood Moons and Two Feasts," in *Four Blood Moons*.
- Read chapter 13, "The Four Blood Moons of 1493–94," in *Four Blood Moons*.
- Read chapter 14, "The Four Blood Moons of 1949–50," in *Four Blood Moons*.

KEY VERSE

I will show wonders in heaven above
And signs in the earth beneath:
Blood and fire and vapor of smoke.
The sun shall be turned into darkness,
And the moon into blood,
Before the coming of the great and awesome day of the Lord.

—ACTS 2:19–20

KEY PASSAGE FROM *FOUR BLOOD MOONS*

Three Tetrads that are specifically linked to Jewish history have appeared in the past five hundred years. Each Tetrad series, consisting of four consecutive Blood Moons with a total solar eclipse occurring somewhere within the sequence of the total lunar eclipses, announced a time of tears and tribulation that would end in national triumph for the Jewish people.

—*Four Blood Moons*, chapter 13

● QUESTIONS FOR PERSONAL STUDY ●

CHAPTER 12: THE FOUR BLOOD MOONS AND TWO FEASTS

Tetrads linked to significant Jewish history have happened only three times in more than five hundred years. These specific occurrences could not be ignored. My further research led me to the unmistakable biblical and scientific truth that they are about to happen a fourth time. (173)

- Based on your study so far, how would you answer Pastor Mark's question now: "Have you ever considered the sun, moon, and stars in the study of prophecy?"

- In the space below, jot down a few of the things you have learned so far in your study of *Four Blood Moons*. And then hang on—you are about to leap out of your chair when you see what God reveals next!

NASA DISCOVERY

The Scriptures speak of "signs in the heavens," many of which have been confirmed by NASA. (172)

- Why is it important to search out what NASA and other scientific organizations have to say about upcoming astronomical events when studying the sun, moon, and stars in relation to prophecy? In what ways could NASA's projections support or debunk a particular interpretation of astronomical events?

- Read Exodus 4:22. What does God call Israel in this verse? How is God's relationship to the nation of Israel relevant to a study of biblical prophecy in connection with the sun, moon, and stars?

- What is very significant about NASA's recorded dates of recent Tetrads (series of Four Blood Moons) in connection with Israel's history? Look at page 172 of *Four Blood Moons* and write the years below. (For now, just write the years. You don't have to know the historical events associated with those years yet; we will study the events this week and in week 8.)

THE ABSOLUTE TRUTH

When I discover a potential new prophetic revelation, I go to the absolute truth of the Word of God, which is the foundation of all sound biblical research and teaching. (173)

- How does Genesis 1:1 sweep away atheism and assert God's all-powerful existence?

- How does God describe Himself in Deuteronomy 6:4? How does this verse confirm that there is only one, true God—and not many pagan gods for us to worship?

- What is God's relationship to the nation of Israel as revealed in Genesis 12:1–3 and Zechariah 12:8? Who created the nation of Israel from the descendants of Abraham? What has God sworn to do for His people?

- What do you learn about His character in Hebrews 13:8? Will God ever change?

THE FEASTS OF THE LORD

Through these festivals, God is giving us a depiction of what He has already done as well as a prophetic portrait of what is coming in the years ahead. (175)

PASSOVER

Passover (Pesach) begins on the 15th day of the Jewish month of Nissan. It is the first of the two major festivals with both historical and agricultural significance that occur in the Tetrad. (176)

- Read Leviticus 23:4–5. When does Passover begin?

- Read Exodus 12:14. What is God's purpose for instituting the feast of Passover?

Pesach

The word *Pesach* comes from the Hebrew root *Pei-Samekh-Cheit*, meaning to pass through, to pass over, to exempt, or to spare. It refers to the tenth and last plague of Egypt, recorded in Exodus 12:1–14. In this event, the angel of the Lord "passed over"—and didn't slay the firstborn son in—the houses of the Jewish people who applied the blood of the lamb to the doorposts. *Pesach* is also the name of a lamb that was sacrificed in the Temple to commemorate this holiday.

- The sacrifice of the Passover lamb is an essential part of the feast. Read the following scriptures and write down any connections you observe between the Passover lamb and Jesus, the Lamb of God:

  John 1:29

  1 Corinthians 5:7

  1 Peter 1:19

  Revelation 5:6–13

The Feast of Passover is a time of redemption. (179)

THE FEAST OF TABERNACLES

The Festival of Tabernacles (Sukkot) begins on the 15th day of the Jewish month of Tishri. (179)

- Read Leviticus 23:24–43 for a full description of this Jewish feast. Write below your insights about this festival.

- How many days does the Feast of Tabernacles last? What were the people to do on both the first day and the eighth day (v. 39)?

- What other significant action were the Jewish people commanded to do on the first day of this feast (v. 40)?

- Where are the Jewish people commanded to live during this festival (v. 42)? Why (v. 43)?

Sukkot

....

The word *Sukkot* means "booths." It refers to the temporary dwellings that the Jewish people were commanded to make and live in during this holiday. The purpose of making these temporary huts, or "booths," during the feast is for the Jewish people to remember that the Israelites lived in similar "booths" during their forty years of wandering in the desert. (See Leviticus 23:42–43.)

....

The Feast of Tabernacles is a time of remembrance, rejoicing, and rest. (181)

For more information on how the Jewish feasts relate to biblical prophecy, turn to part 2 of this study guide and read chapter 15: "How Do the Jewish Feasts Relate to the End Times?"

CHAPTER 13: THE FOUR BLOOD MOONS OF 1493–94

In 1493–94, the first Tetrad of Blood Moons occurred on the Jewish holidays of Passover and Feast of Tabernacles:

1. *Passover, April 2, 1493*
2. *Feast of Tabernacles, September 25, 1493*
3. *Passover, March 22, 1494*
4. *Feast of Tabernacles, September 15, 1494*

... What was happening to the Jewish people during this time? (184)

BLOOD MOONS OF 1493–94

Passover	Total Solar Eclipse	Feast of Tabernacles	Passover	Feast of Tabernacles
April 2, 1493	September 24, 1493	September 25, 1493	March 22, 1494	September 15, 1494

King Ferdinand and Queen Isabella

On March 30, 1492, at their palace in Granada, King Ferdinand and Queen Isabella signed a decree ordering the Jews to leave Castile and Aragon by August 1. This was known as the Edict of Expulsion, which banished all Jewish people from Spain who refused to convert to Catholicism. (187)

- How do you think you would have responded if you were a Jew during the time of the Spanish Inquisition? How might you have felt? What might you have done?

- Why was the Edict of Expulsion so devastating to the Jewish people? What were they forced to leave behind? What could have happened to them on their long journey? How did the edict affect their future?

- The day following the Edict of Expulsion, in the Jewish calendar, was the 9th of Av. Why is this date significant to Jewish history? What have you learned about the 9th of Av so far in our study?

Spanish Inquisition

During the period of church history known as the Inquisition, religious leaders of the organized church segregated, tortured, banished, and killed Jews and others who refused to convert to "Christianity." But as I said in chapter 1, it may have been called *Christianity*, but the acts of the Inquisition had *nothing* to do with actual *Christianity*. They had nothing to do with the love of God. They were *not* connected to our Savior and Lord. These were acts of tyranny by pious church leaders whose souls were poisoned by anti-Semitism. The Inquisition—and other villainous acts of historic Christianity—should never be labeled as something sanctioned by the message of Jesus Christ. Never!

A HARBOR OF REFUGE

God caused Christopher Columbus to discover the "new world," which would eventually become America, a refuge to the Jewish people and all who were oppressed by tyrants and religious dictators around the world. (193)

- Reread God's pledge to Abraham in Genesis 12:3. How does Christopher Columbus's discovery of America as a land of refuge for the Jewish people fulfill God's covenant to Abraham and his descendants?

- In what ways has the nation of America been blessed as a result of protecting and providing for the Jewish people?

- In what ways did the nation of Spain suffer a "curse" as a result of the Edict of Expulsion? Since the edict in 1492, has Spain increased or decreased in power and prosperity? What do you know of current events in Spain? Is Spain considered one of the world's superpowers today? Why or why not?

The expulsion of the Jews from Spain in 1492 was a world-changing moment. The mantle of prosperity was lifted from Spain and placed upon the shoulders of an infant nation that would become the United States of America. God Almighty used the Four Blood Moons of 1493–94 as a heavenly billboard *to mankind.* (195)

CHAPTER 14: THE FOUR BLOOD MOONS OF 1949–50

This Tetrad, beginning in 1949, occurred on the Jewish holidays of Passover and the Feast of Tabernacles:

1. *Passover, April 13, 1949*
2. *Feast of Tabernacles, October 7, 1949*
3. *Passover, April 2, 1950*
4. *Feast of Tabernacles, September 26, 1950*

… What was happening to the Jewish people during this time? (198)

BLOOD MOONS OF 1949–50

Passover	Feast of Tabernacles	Passover	**Total Solar Eclipse**	Feast of Tabernacles
April 13, 1949	October 7, 1949	April 2, 1950	**September 12, 1950**	September 26, 1950

- Read Ezekiel 36:24, 28. In these verses, what does God promise to do for the Jewish people, who had been scattered in exile throughout the world?

It was in 1948 that Israel was once again declared a nation. There is no greater miracle in human history that the miracle of the ingathering of the seed of Abraham. The Land of Israel was the birthplace of the Jewish people. The Land of Israel was where their spiritual identity was shaped. The Land of Israel is where the Jewish people will reside forever. (198–99)

- Why is the statehood of Israel in 1948 considered to be a "miracle"?

- The Jews were forcibly exiled from their homeland in AD 70. How many years had the Jewish people been scattered across the world? If you had been a Jew during these years, do you think you would have held out hope for God to fulfill His promise to Israel in Ezekiel 36? Why or why not?

- How would the declaration of Israel as a state and the ingathering of the Jews back to their homeland in 1948 have affected their faith in God? How does it affect *your* faith in God?

- Read Isaiah 66:8. How was the declaration of Israel as a state in 1948 a fulfillment of this prophecy? How does this verse reveal that the ingathering of Israel could be done only by a sovereign act of Almighty God?

Iyar—the Second Month

Israel was reborn in the month of Iyar—the second month in the Hebrew calendar. This second month holds great biblical significance. It was in the *second month* that King Solomon started building the First Temple (1 Kings 6:1). It was in the *second month* that Ezra began to rebuild the Second Temple (Ezra 3:8). And it was in the *second month* that Israel was reborn as a nation.

It was during this process of Israel's rebirth and the establishment of her borders that on Passover 1949 God splattered the heavens with the first Blood Moon of the second Tetrad. The Jewish people had endured the severe tribulation of the Holocaust, the trials of rebirthing a nation, and now it was a time of triumph; they were officially home and home forever. (206–7)

• QUESTIONS FOR GROUP DISCUSSION •

• What have you learned so far in this study about God's relationship to the Jewish people? Who created the nation of Israel? How does God relate to Israel? Will His attitude and promises toward Israel ever change? What has He promised to do for the Jewish people? Support your insights with Scripture.

• Discuss what you learned this week about the Feast of Passover. What biblical event does Passover commemorate? How is Passover a reminder of God's redemption? How does the feast foretell a coming sacrificial Lamb who will save His people from judgment and death? Now discuss what you learned about the Feast of Tabernacles. Why is this feast significant to the nation of Israel? What does it show us about God's character? If you have time, discuss what you learned about the Jewish Feasts and their correspondence to biblical prophecy in chapter 15, "How Do the Jewish Feasts Relate to the End Times?"

• Why was the Edict of Expulsion in the Spanish Inquisition so devastating to the Jewish people? How did God intervene in this situation? Briefly discuss the edict and the events that followed. How does God's provision of a land of refuge demonstrate His faithfulness to the Jewish people? Do you think the Four Blood Moons of that year are significant? Why or why not?

• Why was the reestablishment of the State of Israel after World War II such a miracle? How is God's hand clearly seen through the events leading up to the declaration of Israel as a nation in 1948? In what ways did this event fulfill biblical prophecy? (Support your answers with Scripture.) How does this historical event demonstrate God's faithfulness to the Jewish people? Do you think the Four Blood Moons of that year are significant? Why or why not?

PRAYER

Heavenly Father, in Your eyes, we know that little piece of property on the edge of the Mediterranean is the most important property in all the world. In Genesis, You made an everlasting covenant with Abraham that the land will belong to Israel forever, and that You would bless anyone who blesses the Jews and curse anyone who curses them. Increase our awareness of Your current relationship with the Jewish people. The set time to favor Israel has arrived, and we want to stand up for and support Israel as You give us opportunity. In the name of Jesus our Messiah, we pray, amen.

Take Action

- Go online to a Jewish calendar website and search for the coming feast days. Write them in your calendar as reminders to pray especially diligently for the nation of Israel on those days. Ask that God would show the Jewish people mercy, that their eyes would be opened, and that God's favor would shine down on them. Pray for the peace of Jerusalem.

- Ask around or search online for a Messianic Jewish synagogue in your area. Attend one of the Shabbat (Sabbath) services to better understand the Jewish people and to demonstrate your support for Israel.

- Ask a Jewish friend to share with you some of his or her personal experiences with anti-Semitism. Ask how you can be a support to him or her as someone who "blesses" those whom God has blessed.

WEEK 8:

The Four Blood Moons of 1967–68 and 2014–15

⚬

Study of Chapters 15–16 in *Four Blood Moons*

....

There will be a fourth series of Four Blood Moons in the
near future. NASA has stated that this will be the last
appearance of a Tetrad in this century. What historical
event will take place during their occurrences that is
significant to Israel and the Jewish people?
More importantly, what is God saying to mankind?
(*Four Blood Moons*, chapter 15)

....

Prepare for Week 8

- Read chapter 15, "The Four Blood Moons of 1967–68," in *Four Blood Moons*.
- Read chapter 16, "The Four Blood Moons of 2014–15," in *Four Blood Moons*.

Key Verse

I have chosen Jerusalem,
that My name may be there.

—2 Chronicles 6:6

Key Passage from *Four Blood Moons*

We're getting ready to leave here. The King is coming! He is coming soon with power and great glory, and His reward is with Him (Isaiah 40:10). Are you ready? Are the members of your family ready? It's the greatest question you will ever answer in this life!

When you see these signs in the heavens, don't be afraid; rather lift up your heads and rejoice. Shout for joy! Your redemption draws nigh. The battle is over; soon we shall wear a robe and a crown of life.

—*Four Blood Moons*, chapter 16

• QUESTIONS FOR PERSONAL STUDY •

CHAPTER 15: THE FOUR BLOOD MOONS OF 1967–68

The Tetrad of Blood Moons of 1967–68 occurred on the Jewish holidays of Passover and the Feast of Tabernacles:

1. *Passover, April 24, 1967*
2. *Feast of Tabernacles, October 18, 1967*
3. *Passover, April 13, 1968*
4. *Feast of Tabernacles, October 6, 1968*
... What was happening to the Jewish people during this time? (210)

BLOOD MOONS OF 1967–68

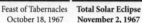

Passover	Feast of Tabernacles	**Total Solar Eclipse**	Passover	Feast of Tabernacles
April 24, 1967	October 18, 1967	**November 2, 1967**	April 13, 1968	October 6, 1968

- Read 2 Chronicles 6:6. Based on this verse, along with your study so far, why is the city of Jerusalem unlike any other city on earth?

THE PRIDE OF INDEPENDENCE

Israel was at war from the moment they declared statehood. (211)

- Read Psalm 83:2–4. What attitudes and actions do Israel's enemies have toward Israel? What is their ultimate goal, according to verse 4?

- Read the description of the events leading up to the Six-Day War, described on pages 211–13 in *Four Blood Moons*. In the space below list the nations who joined together to fight against Israel. Read the quotes from Arab leaders and underline in your book or note below their expressed goal concerning the nation of Israel.

THE HAND OF GOD

The Six-Day War was a war of miracles. God gave Israel triumph after triumph against their ancient enemies that had occupied their land and divided the sacred city of Jerusalem for centuries. There was no military reason for their victory; it was simply the hand of God! (214)

- Read Joshua 4:24. According to this verse, why does God supernaturally intervene in the affairs of His people, Israel?

- Read the eyewitness account of the conquest of Shechem on pages 215–16 of *Four Blood Moons*. How does this event reveal the hand of God?

- In the space below, note a few other events of the Six-Day War, described in chapter 15 of *Four Blood Moons*, that can only be explained as the supernatural intervention of the hand of God, orchestrating the events in favor of the Jewish people.

- The Old City of Jerusalem had been under Jordanian control for nineteen years. But it took just three days for Israeli forces to defeat the Jordanian army. How does this shocking victory relate to the following statement from David Ben-Gurion: "In Israel, in order to be a realist, you must believe in miracles"?

- Read Psalm 14:7. Remember from our study in week 1 that *Zion* refers to Mount Zion, in the city of Jerusalem. Write out the verse in the space below. Put a circle around what God does for Jerusalem. Underline how the people will respond.

- Read Amos 9:14–15. After the Jewish people return to Israel from their second exile, will they ever be removed from their covenant homeland again?

God's signature was on the miraculous victory of the Six-Day War. He signaled this historic event with the third series of Four Blood Moons. The trials and tribulation of war finally brought forth triumph for the Jewish people—the unification of their beloved Jerusalem. (220–21)

CHAPTER 16: THE FOUR BLOOD MOONS OF 2014–15

The next time the Four Blood Moons begin to appear will be in April of 2014. NASA has projected that the Tetrad will begin on April 2014 and end in September 2015. It will occur in the following sequence:

1. *Passover, April 15, 2014*
2. *Feast of Tabernacles, October 8, 2014*

3. *Passover, April 4, 2015*

4. *Feast of Tabernacles, September 28, 2015*

... What is the prophetic significance of these Four Blood Moons? (223–24)

BLOOD MOONS OF 2014–15

Passover	Feast of Tabernacles	**Total Solar Eclipse**	Passover	Feast of Tabernacles
April 15, 2014	October 8, 2014	**March 20, 2015**	April 4, 2015	September 28, 2015

To answer that important question, let's review the journey we've taken so far in our study:

• What were the common denominators of 1492, 1949, and 1967? Write the significant historical events—and their connection to the nation of Israel—in the space below:

    1492:

    1949:

    1967:

• Fill in the blanks below with what you have learned in our study so far:

Each of the three previous series of Four Blood Moons began with a trail of _____ and ended with _____ for the Jewish people. (225)

- Reread the prophecy given in Joel 2:30–31, and repeated in Acts 2:19–20. Then answer these questions:

    What heavenly signs are mentioned in these prophecies?

    When will these signs appear? What future event do they point to?

- According to Luke 21:28, how are we to respond when we see these signs? Why?

I believe that the heavens are God's high-definition billboard. I believe that He has been sending signals and speaking to planet earth in the heavens since creation—we just haven't considered the meaning of the signals. (226)

PROPHETIC BULL'S-EYE

When you set your sites on the signs of the terminal generation and concentrate on the concept of the Shemittah year, then you will clearly see your target, squeeze the trigger, and hit the bull's-eye! (228)

- Read Matthew 24:33–34. What does this verse say about the specific generation alive at the time that "these things" occur?

- Read Genesis 15:13–15. According to verse 14, how many years will Abraham's descendants be slaves in Egypt ("strangers in a land that is not theirs")? Then according to verse 16, how many generations have passed during that time? How many years are considered "one generation" in God's timetable?

• In His Olivet Discourse (Matthew 24), Jesus tells His disciples that when we see the signs of the terminal generation, *that* generation will see His return in the clouds of heaven. Based on what you have learned so far in our study, do you believe we are that generation? Why or why not?

Terminal Generation

The word *terminal* means "concluding" or "constituting the end of a period or series."[1] In theological terms, the phrase *terminal generation* refers to the generation that will be alive on the earth when Jesus raptures His church, an event that launches the seven-year Great Tribulation described by Jesus in the Olivet Discourse and by the apostle John in the book of Revelation.

Signs of the Terminal Generation

We can't deny [the signs of the terminal generation's] existence and their importance to the next series of Blood Moons. (229)

• Look at the following list of the Signs of the Terminal Generation. Beside each item on the list, write whether the sign has been fulfilled yet:

1. Rebirth of Israel
2. The Ingathering

3. Jewish control of Jerusalem
4. Deception on a global scale
5. The resurrection of the Hebrew language
6. The knowledge explosion
7. The birth of nuclear warfare

- Look at your answers on the list above. What do they reveal to you about the likelihood that we are currently living in the terminal generation? Is it possible that the "terminal generation" began when Israel was reborn in 1948—and that we are living within that generation, according to God's timetable?

THE SHEMITTAH YEAR
Every seven years we experience a Shemittah year in which God allows something to happen that gets our undivided attention whether we are ready or not! (233)

- Review the list of Shemittah years on page 234 of *Four Blood Moons* and write below a brief description of the significant event that happened on each of those years:

  Shemittah year of 1973:

  Shemittah year of 1980:

  Shemittah year of 1987:

  Shemittah year of 1994:

Shemittah year of 2001:

Shemittah year of 2008:

- What significant event could possibly happen in the Shemittah year of 2015? Remember, God does everything at a "set time" (Psalm 102:13).

THE FEAST OF TRUMPETS
This holiday is . . . a day of remembrance or the day of sounding of the shofar. It is called the Feast of Trumpets. (237)

Shofar
A shofar is a ram's horn that sounds like a trumpet. Some Jewish people believe that the sounding of the shofar is the call to repentance.

- Read Leviticus 23:24–25. What do you learn from these verses about the Jewish Feast of Trumpets? How is this feast day to be celebrated?

- Look carefully at the graphic below. What do you notice about the Feast of Trumpets and the Feast of Tabernacles in 2014?

| Passover April 15, 2014 | Rosh Hashanah Feast of Trumpets September 25, 2014 | Feast of Tabernacles October 8, 2014 | **Total Solar Eclipse March 20, 2015** | Passover April 4, 2015 | Rosh Hashanah Feast of Trumpets September 13, 2015 | Feast of Tabernacles September 28, 2015 |

The Shemittah year and the Feast of Tabernacles begin at sunset September 25, 2014. These occurrences are not coincidental! This is the hand of God orchestrating the signs in the heavens. (237)

Rosh Hashanah

Rosh Hashanah occurs on the first and second days of the Jewish month of Tishri. In Hebrew, *Rosh Hashanah* means "head of the year" or "first of the year." Rosh Hashanah is commonly known as the Jewish New Year and is a time of reflection and introspection.

- Read Micah 7:19. Based on this verse, some Jews adopted the practice of *Tashlikh*, or "casting off," where they walk through flowing water and empty their pockets into the river, beginning the New Year by symbolically casting off their sins. What "rocks in your pocket" do you need to cast off into the ever-flowing river of God's forgiveness today? What sins are weighing you down that need to be confessed and repented of? Take time to do it now! Your new year—and new life—can begin today.

ISRAEL'S HOSTILE NEIGHBORS

Israel's enemies can be divided into two groups: the surrounding Islamic nations that have historically been their opponents in past wars, and radical terrorist organizations formed more recently that are committed to Israel's destruction. (240)

- Read pages 241–43 in *Four Blood Moons*, and then write below any insights you learn about each of Israel's enemies, gathering together even now against the nation of Israel:

Egypt:

Syria:

Jordan:

Iran:

Radical Islamic organizations:
(PLO, Hamas, Hezbollah, Fatah)

• How are we seeing 1967 repeat itself all over again as we look at Israel's current enemies? In what ways are their enemies the same—and perhaps even stronger? What is their ultimate goal regarding the nation of Israel?

• Based on what you have learned so far in our study of biblical prophecy, Scripture promises, and history, how do you think God will respond to another attack on Israel by her enemies?

ARE YOU READY?

God is getting ready to change the course of human history once again. He is preparing to display the next series of signs in the heavens. What is going to happen? The question is not about the terminal generation or when Israel's enemies are going to attack next—the question is are you ready to meet the Lord? Are your children ready? (244)

- What are your honest answers to these important questions? Write them out in the space provided below.

   Are you ready to meet the Lord?

   Are your children ready?

- If you are not ready, what steps can you take—*right now*—to get ready to meet the Lord when He catches us up together with Him in the clouds at the Rapture?

The coming Four Blood Moons are almost here . . . are you ready? (246)

• QUESTIONS FOR GROUP DISCUSSION •

- What did you learn about God and His relationship to Israel as you studied the Six-Day War this week? What specific events stood out to you? What insights did you gain into the Bible and God's character as you studied the events leading up to and surrounding the Six-Day War?

- Look at the list of signs of the terminal generation. What do these signs tell us about the possibility that we are the last generation to live on earth before Christ returns to rapture His church? How does the realization of Christ's imminent return make you feel—excited? afraid? nervous? joyous? Describe your emotions to the group. If you are feeling afraid, examine yourself to see whether you are in the faith (2 Corinthians

13:5). If you aren't, what are you waiting for? Trust in Christ *today!* If you do belong to God, then lift up your heads and rejoice. Shout for joy! Your redemption draws nigh. The battle is over; soon we shall wear a robe and a crown of life!

- Read the following and discuss as a group: *We're getting ready to leave here. The King is coming! He is coming soon with power and great glory, and His reward is with Him (Isaiah 40:10). Are you ready? Are the members of your family ready? It's the greatest question you will ever answer in this life!* (244)

- If you have time, read through and discuss chapter 16, "Frequently Asked Questions about *Four Blood Moons.*"

PRAYER

May we walk away from this study in the absolute confidence that all of our tomorrows are totally in God's hand, and no one can take us out of His hand. We are sheltered in the arms of God. We are God's people, and God is our defense, He is our fortress, He is our high tower, He is our shield, He is our buckler. Nothing can come to us that God does not permit, therefore we rejoice and remain faithful to the King of kings and the Lord of lords. May we go forth and walk in the confidence that we are children of God, and when the trumpet of God sounds, we are prepared to see the King in all of His glory. Amen.

TAKE ACTION

- In this study, you have discovered that God uses the sun, moon, and stars as His high-definition billboard, announcing future events in relation to His people, Israel. You have read of ways to take action about the information you have learned in this book. Take time now to write out what you feel God would have you do in light of this information.

- Go back through the Take Action suggestions in weeks 1–7 and review them. Is there something you haven't yet done? Make a plan to do it now! Don't let this opportunity pass you by.

- Resolve and commit before God to establish a plan and walk in it so you are prepared to leave a legacy for your loved ones and ready to escape the coming turmoil when Jesus returns to rapture His church. Since we do not know the day or the hour of His return (Matthew 24:36), what do you need to do to be prepared?

PART TWO

DIGGING DEEPER

What Does the Bible Say about Astronomy versus Astrology?

There may be some people using this companion study guide and journal who are unsure of the difference between astronomy and astrology. In this brief chapter, I will explain the contrasts between the two studies, and then give you a glimpse of what the Bible says about each one.

ASTRONOMY

WHAT IS ASTRONOMY?

Astronomy is the science of studying the movements and positions of celestial objects such as the sun, moon, stars, planets, and other objects in space. For example, the science of astronomy has taught us that the North Star never moves. Knowing where the North Star is has helped captains of ships chart their courses and sail the seven seas of earth for centuries.

The science of astronomy has enabled us to learn more about the universe and even send people to the moon! Astronomy involves methodical, scientific observations of the night sky, tracing the patterns and orbits of celestial objects and thus predicting, based on factual data, future cosmic events such as solar and lunar eclipses.

WHAT DOES THE BIBLE SAY ABOUT ASTRONOMY?

When it comes to the subject of astronomy, the most important thing the Bible tells us about the heavenly bodies is that God created them. The book of Genesis describes God's creation of the sun, moon, and stars:

> In the beginning God created the heavens and the earth . . .
>
> Then God said, "Let there be lights in the firmament of the heavens to *divide the day from the night*; and *let them be for signs and seasons*, and *for days and years*; and let them be for lights in the firmament of the heavens to *give light on the earth*"; and it was so. Then God made two great lights: the greater light to rule the day, and the lesser light to rule the night. He made the stars also. God set them in the firmament of the heavens to give light on the earth, and to rule over the day and over the night, and to divide the light from the darkness. And God saw that it was good.
>
> —GENESIS 1:1, 14–18

In this passage, we can observe God's four stated purposes for the heavenly bodies:

1. to divide the day from the night
2. to be for signs and for seasons
3. to be for days and years
4. to give light to the earth.

God created the sun to rule the day, the moon to rule the night, and the stars to fill the sky. This passage also tells us the stars were given for "seasons" and "for days and years"—that is, they were given to mark time for us. They also "give light" to us so we don't have to live in darkness.

Interestingly, the word "signs" in Genesis 1:14 comes from the Hebrew word *owth,* meaning "signals." So God is saying early on in Genesis that He uses the heavens to communicate with people.

The Bible also says that the heavens are the work of God's hands:

I consider Your heavens, *the work of Your fingers,*
The moon and the stars, which You have ordained.

—PSALM 8:3

The heavens declare the glory of God;
And the firmament shows *His handiwork.*
Day unto day utters speech,
And night unto night reveals knowledge.
There is no speech nor language
Where their voice is not heard.
Their line has gone out through all the earth,
And their words to the end of the world.

—PSALM 19:1–4

Notice that when King David wrote Psalm 19, he said that the heavens are not only created by God, but they were created with a purpose: They have a "voice" and "declare the glory of God" to the entire world. They also "reveal knowledge" to those who are watching them. So according to the Word of God, it is clear that there is a communication from heaven to man via the sun, moon, planets, and stars formed by our Creator God.

How many stars are in the universe? The number of stars is so large that even the world's greatest scientific minds can't be certain.

But the Bible says that God knows exactly how many stars are in the heavens—and astoundingly, He calls them all by name!

> He counts the number of the stars;
> He calls them all by name.
>
> —PSALM 147:4

In fact, the number of stars that God created is so vast that when God made a covenant with Abraham and promised to bring forth from his son Isaac a great nation with many descendants, He used the stars as an illustration of just how large the number of Jewish people would be someday (Genesis 15:5). In doing so, God was encouraging Abraham to look up at the sky every night for a reminder of His covenant and faithfulness. Does God want us to study the stars in relationship to His Word and look into the heavens as a reminder of His sovereign creative power and everlasting faithfulness? Yes!

God's Word also says that the "day of the Lord"—the final judgment of the earth—will be accompanied by astronomical events relating to the stars.

> Behold, the day of the LORD comes,
> Cruel, with both wrath and fierce anger,
> To lay the land desolate;
> And He will destroy its sinners from it.
> For the stars of heaven and their constellations
> Will not give their light;
> The sun will be darkened in its going forth,

And the moon will not cause its light to shine.

—Isaiah 13:9–10

The day of the Lord is near in the valley of decision.
The sun and moon will grow dark,
And the stars will diminish their brightness.

—Joel 3:14–15

Immediately after the tribulation of those days the sun will be darkened, and the moon will not give its light; the stars will fall from heaven, and the powers of the heavens will be shaken. Then the sign of the Son of Man will appear in heaven.

—Matthew 24:29–30

And, as we have seen in our study of the Four Blood Moons, the Bible is clear that the sun, moon, and stars are sources of prophetic direction, as prophesied in Joel 2:30–31:

And I will show wonders in the heavens and in the earth:
Blood and fire and pillars of smoke.
The sun shall be turned into darkness,
And the moon into blood,
Before the coming of the great and awesome day of the Lord.

The apostle Peter, on the Day of Pentecost, made nearly the exact same remarks, as recorded in Acts 2:19–20:

I will show wonders in heaven above
And signs in the earth beneath:
Blood and fire and vapor of smoke.
The sun shall be turned into darkness,
And the moon into blood,
Before the coming of the great and awesome day of the Lord.

Does the Bible have anything to say about how Christians should view the sun, moon, and stars? Is it okay to study them? Does God permit us looking at the stars to watch for signs of His coming? Again, according to the words of Jesus Christ Himself, the answer is *yes!*

When Jesus' disciples asked Him how they could know when the time of His return would come, Jesus told them to look up at the stars. He said:

There will be signs in the sun, in the moon, and in the stars. . . . Now when these things begin to happen, *look up and lift up your heads*, because your redemption draws near.

—LUKE 21:25, 28

ASTROLOGY

WHAT IS ASTROLOGY?

Astrology is the worship of stars, which is occultism and pagan. People who make choices based on the stars are seeking guidance for their lives from things created rather than from the Creator. This is a violation of the Law of Almighty God (Romans 1:20–21; Exodus 20:4).

Astrology does more than simply study the facts and patterns of the stars; it goes a step further and imposes an imaginary interpretation of how the stars and planets supposedly influence a person's life and destiny.

WHAT DOES THE BIBLE SAY ABOUT ASTROLOGY?

The Bible is clear that astrology is a false belief, with no power to tell the future or make accurate interpretations. When the king of Babylon sought men with wisdom and understanding, all the magicians and astrologers were put to shame by God's prophet Daniel (Daniel 1:20).

When the king later had a disturbing dream, he called upon the royal astrologers to interpret his dream. But the astrologers were shown to be frauds when they admitted they were only able to come up with an interpretation of the dream if the king first revealed the dream to them. Infuriated to discover that his astrologists were charlatans, the king called upon Daniel, who declared:

> The secret which the king has demanded, the wise men, the astrologers, the magicians, and the soothsayers cannot declare to the king. But there is a God in heaven who reveals secrets."
>
> —DANIEL 2:27–28

God gives a strong warning to His people against worshipping the stars instead of worshipping the Creator of the stars:

> Take heed, lest you lift your eyes to heaven, and when you see the sun, the moon, and the stars, all the host of heaven, you feel driven to worship them and serve them, which the LORD your God has given to all the peoples under the whole heaven as a heritage.
>
> —DEUTERONOMY 4:19

When astrology is used as an act of sorcery and divination (fortune-telling), God labels the practice an "abomination" and expressly forbids His people from participating in such things:

> There shall not be found among you anyone who makes his son or his daughter pass through the fire, or one who practices witchcraft, or a soothsayer, or one who interprets omens, or a sorcerer, or one who conjures spells, or a medium, or a spiritist, or one who calls up the dead. For all who do these things are an abomination to the LORD, and because of these abominations the LORD your God drives them out from before you. You shall be blameless before the LORD your God. For these nations which you will dispossess listened to soothsayers and diviners; but as for you, the LORD your God has not appointed such for you.
>
> —DEUTERONOMY 18:10–14

In Isaiah 47:13–14, God includes astrologers and stargazers among those who will be unable to save God's people and, as a consequence for their sinful behavior, be burned "as stubble" in His judgment:

Let now the astrologers, the stargazers,
And the monthly prognosticators
Stand up and save you
From what shall come upon you.
Behold, they shall be as stubble,
The fire shall burn them;
They shall not deliver themselves
From the power of the flame;
It shall not be a coal to be warmed by,
Nor a fire to sit before!

Despite these strong warnings from God, several times throughout their history the Jewish people practiced the sin of astrology. One example of star worship, followed by God's judgment, is given in 2 Kings 17:16–18:

They bowed down to all the starry hosts. . . .They practiced
divination and sought omens and sold themselves to do evil
in the eyes of the LORD, arousing his anger. So the LORD was
very angry with Israel and removed them from his presence
(NIV).

A BIBLICAL APPROACH TO THE SUN, MOON, AND STARS

So how should Christians respond to the sun, moon, and stars?

When we look up at the heavens, we should marvel at God's magnificent power and worship Him. We should use the sun for light and warmth during the day, and the moon and stars for light during the night. We should observe the patterns of the stars to mark time and seasons, and to chart navigational courses. We should read the Scriptures to understand the signs that God has written into the stars and carefully observe the heavens for fulfillment of those biblical prophecies.

Most of all, we should respond to the stars by looking up and worshipping the Creator of the sun, moon, and stars.

10

Are There Other Biblical Prophecies Involving the Sun, Moon, and Stars?

The Bible is clear that God created the sun, moon, and stars (Genesis 1:1, 14–18) and that He has absolute control over these celestial bodies (Psalm 147:4). King David goes on to explain that the stars have a "voice" that "declare" God's work to Israel and to all the nations of the world (Psalm 19:1–4).

Throughout history, God has used the sun, moon, and stars as His heavenly billboard pointing to future events, outlined in biblical prophecy. In this chapter, I will give you ten Bible prophecies that involve the sun, moon, and stars.

1. Behold, the day of the LORD comes,
    Cruel, with both wrath and fierce anger,
    To lay the land desolate;
    And He will destroy its sinners from it.
    For the stars of heaven and their constellations
    Will not give their light;
    The sun will be darkened in its going forth,
    And the moon will not cause its light to shine.
    —ISAIAH 13:9–10

2. "When I put out your light,
    I will cover the heavens, and make its stars dark;
    I will cover the sun with a cloud,

And the moon shall not give her light.

All the bright lights of the heavens I will make dark over you,

And bring darkness upon your land,"

Says the Lord GOD.

—EZEKIEL 32:7–8

3. The earth quakes before them,

The heavens tremble;

The sun and moon grow dark,

And the stars diminish their brightness.

The LORD gives voice before His army,

For His camp is very great;

For strong is the One who executes His word.

For the day of the LORD is great and very terrible;

Who can endure it?

—JOEL 2:10–11

4. It shall come to pass afterward

That I will pour out My Spirit on all flesh;

Your sons and your daughters shall prophesy,

Your old men shall dream dreams,

Your young men shall see visions.

And also on My menservants and on My maidservants

I will pour out My Spirit in those days.

And I will show wonders in the heavens and in the earth:

Blood and fire and pillars of smoke.
The sun shall be turned into darkness,
And the moon into blood,
Before the coming of the great and awesome day of the LORD.

—JOEL 2:28–31

5. "And it shall come to pass in that day," says the Lord GOD,
   "That I will make the sun go down at noon,
   And I will darken the earth in broad daylight."

—AMOS 8:9

6. Now after Jesus was born in Bethlehem of Judea in the days of Herod the king, behold, wise men from the East came to Jerusalem, saying, "Where is He who has been born King of the Jews? For we have seen His star in the East and have come to worship Him."

When Herod the king heard this, he was troubled, and all Jerusalem with him. And when he had gathered all the chief priests and scribes of the people together, he inquired of them where the Christ was to be born.

So they said to him, "In Bethlehem of Judea, for thus it is written by the prophet:

'But you, Bethlehem, in the land of Judah,
Are not the least among the rulers of Judah;
For out of you shall come a Ruler
Who will shepherd My people Israel.'"

Then Herod, when he had secretly called the wise men, determined from them what time the star appeared. And he sent them to Bethlehem and said, "Go and search carefully for the young Child, and when you have found Him, bring back word to me, that I may come and worship Him also."

When they heard the king, they departed; and behold, the star which they had seen in the East went before them, till it came and stood over where the young Child was. When they saw the star, they rejoiced with exceedingly great joy. And when they had come into the house, they saw the young Child with Mary His mother, and fell down and worshiped Him. And when they had opened their treasures, they presented gifts to Him: gold, frankincense, and myrrh.

—MATTHEW 2:1–11

7. For as the lightning comes from the east and flashes to the west, so also will the coming of the Son of Man be. For wherever the carcass is, there the eagles will be gathered together.

Immediately after the tribulation of those days the sun will be darkened, and the moon will not give its light; the stars will fall from heaven, and the powers of the heavens will be shaken. Then the sign of the Son of Man will appear in heaven, and then all the tribes of the earth will mourn, and they will see the Son of Man coming on the clouds of heaven with power and great glory.

—MATTHEW 24:27–30

8. And there will be signs in the sun, in the moon, and in the stars; and on the earth distress of nations, with perplexity, the sea and the waves roaring; men's hearts failing them from fear and the expectation of those things which are coming on the earth, for the powers of the heavens will be shaken. Then they will see the Son of Man coming in a cloud with power and great glory. Now when these things begin to happen, look up and lift up your heads, because your redemption draws near.

—LUKE 21:25–28

9. And it shall come to pass in the last days, says God,
    That I will pour out of My Spirit on all flesh;
    Your sons and your daughters shall prophesy,
    Your young men shall see visions,
    Your old men shall dream dreams.
    And on My menservants and on My maidservants

I will pour out My Spirit in those days;
And they shall prophesy.
I will show wonders in heaven above
And signs in the earth beneath:
Blood and fire and vapor of smoke.
The sun shall be turned into darkness,
And the moon into blood,
Before the coming of the great and awesome day of the Lord.
And it shall come to pass
That whoever calls on the name of the Lord
Shall be saved.'

—Acts 2:17–21

10. I looked when He opened the sixth seal, and behold, there was a great earthquake; and the sun became black as sackcloth of hair, and the moon became like blood. And the stars of heaven fell to the earth, as a fig tree drops its late figs when it is shaken by a mighty wind. Then the sky receded as a scroll when it is rolled up, and every mountain and island was moved out of its place. And the kings of the earth, the great men, the rich men, the commanders, the mighty men, every slave and every free man, hid themselves in the caves and in the rocks of the mountains, and said to the mountains and rocks, "Fall on us and hide us from the face of Him who sits on the throne and from the wrath of the Lamb! For the great day of His wrath has come, and who is able to stand?"

—Revelation 6:12–17

11

Why Is Jerusalem Significant to God's Plan?

Jerusalem is unlike any other city on the face of the earth. Jerusalem is the place God chose to build His holy temple. It is the homeland of God's chosen people, the Jews. It is the site of God's future kingdom.

Jerusalem is the apple of God's eye—and it will remain the center of the universe for the future of the world! There is not now, and will never be, another city on planet earth like Jerusalem.

JERUSALEM IS THE CITY OF GOD

The Bible is clear that Jerusalem is the city of God. Scripture reveals to us that God has put His holy name on Jerusalem. God says,

And to his son [Solomon] I will give one tribe, that My servant David may always have a lamp before Me in Jerusalem, the city which *I have chosen for Myself, to put My name there.*

—1 KINGS 11:36

I have chosen Jerusalem, *that My name may be there.*

—2 CHRONICLES 6:6

In this house [the Temple] and in Jerusalem, which I have chosen out of all the tribes of Israel, *I will put My name forever.*

—2 CHRONICLES 33:7

If all the forces of hell could drive the Jewish people into extinction, then the name of God would be dishonored. That cannot —and *will not*—happen. Almighty God will protect His name and His glory, which He has placed in the city of Jerusalem.

God says He created Israel. He is the Defender of Israel. He is the One who keeps Israel, and He never slumbers or sleeps. God is on guard, keeping and watching over the nation of Israel, and especially the city that bears His holy name.

In addition to being the city that bears God's name, Jerusalem is also the city where God's presence dwells on earth:

> I have chosen and sanctified this house, that My name may
> be there forever; and *My eyes and My heart will be there
> perpetually*.
>
> —2 CHRONICLES 7:16

Does that mean that God is *only* present in Jerusalem? Of course not. God is not bound by the earth's limits of geographic space—He is present everywhere throughout the earth at all times. However, Scripture is clear that God says He has given Jerusalem a special anointing of His presence.

I have traveled all over the world and have had the opportunity to visit many of the world's greatest and most influential cities. But whenever I am in Jerusalem I sense a unique and powerful presence of the living God of Abraham, Isaac, and Jacob. God established His special presence in Jerusalem through King David, as recorded in Scripture.

Many of the psalms speak of the reality and blessing of God's presence in the city of Jerusalem.

Great is the LORD, and greatly to be praised
In the city of our God,
In His holy mountain.
Beautiful in elevation,
The joy of the whole earth,
Is Mount Zion on the sides of the north,
The city of the great King. . . .
In the city of the LORD of hosts,
In the city of our God:
God will establish it forever.

—PSALM 48:1–2, 8

For the LORD has chosen Zion;
He has desired it for His dwelling place.

—PSALM 132:13

Jerusalem is the heart of Israel. Israel without Jerusalem would be like a human body without a heart. King David expresses well the passionate importance of this city to the Jewish people:

If I forget you, O Jerusalem,
Let my right hand forget its skill!
If I do not remember you,

Let my tongue cling to the roof of my mouth—
If I do not exalt Jerusalem
Above my chief joy.

—Psalm 137:5–6

Let it be known to all people of all nations: The city of Jerusalem belongs to Almighty God and His chosen people, the Jews. The city that bears God's name is not up for negotiation with anyone at any time for any reason in the future. Jerusalem has been—and shall always be—the eternal and undivided capital of the State of Israel.

Jerusalem Is the City of Peace

The name *Jerusalem* literally means "teaching of peace" or "city of peace." *Salem* is associated with the Hebrew word *shalom*, a word that not only means "peace" but also connotes wholeness and completeness.

Salem—meaning "peaceful"—was an early name for the city of Jerusalem.

In Salem [Jerusalem] also is His tabernacle,
And His dwelling place in Zion.

—Psalm 76:2

The Bible also mentions *Salem* in Genesis 14:18, a passage that records "Melchizedek king of *Salem*" giving a blessing to Abraham:

Then Melchizedek king of Salem [Jerusalem] brought out bread and wine; he was the priest of God Most High. And he blessed him and said:

> "Blessed be Abram of God Most High,
> Possessor of heaven and earth;
> And blessed be God Most High,
> Who has delivered your enemies into your hand."
>
> —GENESIS 14:18–20

Yet, despite its name as "the city of peace," Jerusalem has been anything but peaceful throughout history. The citizens of Jerusalem were taken captive by the Babylonians. The Temple was desecrated and the people of Jerusalem murdered by the Romans. Even today, Jerusalem is the center of terrorist threats and political maneuvering.

Lasting peace will not come to Jerusalem until Jesus, the Messiah, comes to usher in the golden age of peace—His millennial kingdom, which will be headquartered in the city of Jerusalem. Scripture describes how the nations of the earth will come up to Jerusalem to worship King Jesus:

> The LORD of hosts will reign
> On Mount Zion and in Jerusalem
> And before His elders, gloriously.
>
> —ISAIAH 24:23

And it shall come to pass that everyone who is left of all the nations which came against Jerusalem shall go up from year to year to worship the King, the LORD of hosts.

—ZECHARIAH 14:16

At that time every man "shall beat their swords into plowshares" and study war no more (Isaiah 2:4). The lion shall lie down with the lamb, and the River of Life shall flow from the Temple Mount to the Dead Sea, nourishing trees that will produce healing for the nations (Revelation 22:1–2).

JERUSALEM IS THE CITY OF JESUS

Jerusalem is the city that Jesus loved. Jesus sat on the side of the Mount of Olives and wept over Jerusalem, saying:

O Jerusalem, Jerusalem, the one who kills the prophets and stones those who are sent to her! How often I wanted to gather your children together, as a hen gathers her chicks under her wings, but you were not willing! See! Your house is left to you desolate; for I say to you, you shall see Me no more till you say, "Blessed is He who comes in the name of the Lord!"

—MATTHEW 23:37–39

As Jesus carried His cross through the streets of Jerusalem on His way to the Crucifixion, He saw women weeping for Him. He stopped, looked tenderly into their faces, and said:

Daughters of Jerusalem, do not weep for Me, but weep for yourselves and for your children. For indeed the days are coming in which they will say, "Blessed are the barren, wombs that never bore, and breasts which never nursed!"

—LUKE 23:28–29

This devastating prophecy was fulfilled just thirty-seven years after Jesus uttered those words, when General Titus and the Roman army besieged the city, demolished the Temple, and destroyed Jerusalem.

But God will keep His promise to restore the Jewish people and His chosen city, Jerusalem!

JERUSALEM IS THE FUTURE OF ISRAEL

The restoration of Jerusalem has already begun. On May 14, 1948, the State of Israel was proclaimed by David Ben-Gurion. It was the day of greatest prophetic fulfillment in the twentieth century. The restoration of Israel happened just as God promised it would through His prophets:

Fear not, for I am with you;
I will bring your descendants from the east,
And gather you from the west;
I will say to the north, "Give them up!"
And to the south, "Do not keep them back!"
Bring My sons from afar,
And My daughters from the ends of the earth.

—ISAIAH 43:5–6

Thus says the Lord GOD: "I will gather you from the peoples, assemble you from the countries where you have been scattered, and I will give you the land of Israel." . . . Then I will give them one heart, and I will put a new spirit within them.

—EZEKIEL 11:17, 19

Again I will build you [Jerusalem], and you shall be rebuilt. . . .
Behold, I will bring them from the north country,
And gather them from the ends of the earth,
Among them the blind and the lame,
The woman with child
And the one who labors with child, together;
A great throng shall return there.

—JEREMIAH 31:4, 8

In anticipation of this great day, King David wrote:

When the LORD brought back the captivity of Zion,
We were like those who dream.
Then our mouth was filled with laughter,
And our tongue with singing.
Then they said among the nations,
"The LORD has done great things for them."

—PSALM 126:1-2

The rebirth of the nation of Israel, and the reestablishment of Jerusalem as its capital, is a prelude to the return of the Lord. The Bible says,

> When the LORD shall build up Zion [Jerusalem], he shall appear in his glory.
>
> —PSALM 102:16 KJV

Scripture makes it clear: when the Lord returns, it will be to the city of Jerusalem, inhabited by the Jewish people!

Why Should Christians Support Israel?

Everything Christians do should be based upon the biblical text. Here are seven solid, biblical reasons that Bible-believing Christians must speak out and stand up for Israel.

1. ISRAEL IS THE ONLY NATION CREATED BY GOD HIMSELF.
Christians should support Israel because all other nations were created by an act of men, but Israel was created by an act of God! As Creator of heaven and earth, God has the ownership and right to give the land to anyone He chooses.

As owner of all the earth, God gave the Royal Land Grant for the land of Israel to Abraham, Isaac, and Jacob and their descendants forever:

> The LORD appeared to Abram and said to him, "I am Almighty God; walk before Me and be blameless. And I will make My covenant between Me and you, and will multiply you exceedingly." Then Abram fell on his face, and God talked with him, saying: "As for Me, behold, My covenant is with you, and you shall be a father of many nations. No longer shall your name be called Abram, but your name shall be Abraham; for I have made you a father of many nations. I will make you exceedingly fruitful; and I will make nations of you, and kings shall come from you. And *I will establish My covenant between Me and you and your*

descendants after you in their generations, for an everlasting covenant, to be God to you and your descendants after you. Also I give to you and your descendants after you the land in which you are a stranger, all the land of Canaan, as an everlasting possession; and I will be their God."

—GENESIS 17:1–8

God repeatedly stated throughout Scripture that the land of Israel belongs to the descendants of Abraham through Isaac and Jacob (Genesis 12:1–3; 13:14–18; 15:1–21; 17:4–8; 22:15–18; 26:1–5). This Royal Land Grant was given to Abraham and his seed, Isaac and Jacob, as an everlasting and unconditional covenant. Notice that Ishmael, the father of the Arab people, was not included in the Royal Land Grant, as clarified by God Himself in Genesis 17:18–21:

And Abraham said to God, "Oh, that Ishmael might live before You!"

Then God said: "No, Sarah your wife shall bear you a son, and you shall call his name Isaac; I will establish My covenant with him for an everlasting covenant, and with his descendants after him. And as for Ishmael, I have heard you. Behold, I have blessed him, and will make him fruitful, and will multiply him exceedingly. He shall beget twelve princes, and I will make him a great nation. But My covenant I will establish with Isaac, whom Sarah shall bear to you at this set time next year."

This promise that God made to Abraham about Ishmael came to pass. The Arab nations, wealthy in oil, are greatly multiplied. However, the descendants of Ishmael do not have a biblical claim of ownership over the land.

God is the creator of Israel—forever the center of the universe.

2. WITHOUT THE JEWISH CONTRIBUTION TO CHRISTIANITY, THERE WOULD BE NO CHRISTIANITY.

The apostle Paul said, "If the Gentiles have been partakers of their [the Jews'] spiritual things, their duty is also to minister to them in material things" (Romans 15:27).

Christians owe a debt of eternal gratitude to the Jewish people for their contributions that gave birth to the Christian faith. Jesus Himself said, "Salvation is of the Jews" (John 4:22). Consider what the Jewish people have given to Christianity:

- The sacred Scripture
- The prophets
- The patriarchs
- Mary, Joseph, and Jesus of Nazareth
- The twelve disciples
- The apostles

It is not possible to say, "I am a Christian," and not love the Jewish people. The Bible teaches that love is not what you say, but what you do (1 John 3:18).

3. JESUS CONSIDERED THE JEWISH PEOPLE HIS FAMILY.

While some Christians try to deny the connection between Jesus of Nazareth and the Jewish people, Jesus never denied His Jewishness. He was born Jewish. He was circumcised on the eighth day in keeping with Jewish tradition. He had His Bar Mitzvah on His thirteenth birthday. He kept the Law of Moses. He wore the prayer shawl that Moses commanded all Jewish men to wear. He died on a cross with the inscription over His head, "King of the Jews."

Jesus considered the Jewish people His family. Jesus said, "Assuredly, I say to you, inasmuch as you did it to one of the least of these My brethren [the Jewish people], you did it to Me" (Matthew 25:40).

4. GOD PROMISED TO BLESS THOSE WHO BLESS ISRAEL AND CURSE THOSE WHO CURSE ISRAEL.

God pledged to Abraham and to his descendants, the Jewish people: "I will bless those who bless you, and I will curse him who curses you; and in you all the families of the earth shall be blessed" (Genesis 12:3).

God has promised to bless the individual or the nation that blesses His chosen people.

History has proven beyond reasonable doubt that the nations that have blessed the Jewish people have received the blessing of God, while the nations that have cursed the Jewish people have experienced the curse of God.

5. CHRISTIANS ARE TO PRAY FOR THE PEACE OF JERUSALEM.
King David tells us:

> Pray for the peace of Jerusalem:
> "May they prosper who love you.
> Peace be within your walls,
> Prosperity within your palaces."

—PSALM 122:6–7

Praying for the peace of Israel isn't a request; it's a command! The scriptural principle of prosperity is tied to blessing the nation of Israel and the city of Jerusalem.

6. GOD REWARDS GENTILES FOR THEIR MINISTRY TO THE JEWS.
Why did Jesus Christ go to the house of a Roman centurion in Capernaum and heal his servant, who was ready to die? What logic did the Jewish elders use with Jesus to convince Him to come into the house of a Gentile and perform a miracle?

The logic they used is recorded in Luke 7:5: "for he loves our nation, and has built us a synagogue." The message? This Gentile deserves the blessing of God because he loves our nation and has done something practical to help the Jewish people.

Why did God the Father select the house of Cornelius in Caesarea to be the first Gentile house in Israel to receive the gospel? The answer is given repeatedly in Acts 10:

- v. 2: He was "a devout man and one who feared God with all his household, who gave alms generously to the people [the Jews]."

- v. 4: The angel said to him, "Your prayers and your alms have come up for a memorial before God."

- vv. 30–31: Cornelius said, "I prayed in my house, and behold, a man stood before me in bright clothing, and said, 'Cornelius, your prayer has been heard, and your alms are remembered in the sight of God.'"

The point is made three times in the same chapter. A godly Gentile who expressed his unconditional love for the Jewish people in a practical manner was divinely selected by heaven to be the first Gentile house to receive the gospel and the first to receive the outpouring of the Holy Spirit.

These combined scriptures verify that *prosperity* (Genesis 12:3; Psalm 122:6), *healing* (Luke 7:1–5), and the *outpouring of the Holy Spirit* (Acts 10) came first to Gentiles who blessed the Jewish people and the nation of Israel in a practical manner.

7. GOD JUDGES GENTILES FOR THEIR MISTREATMENT OF THE JEWS.

Where are the Medo-Persians? Where are the Babylonians? Where are the Greeks? Where is the Roman Empire? Where are the Turks of the Ottoman Empire? Where are Adolf Hitler and his evil, goose-stepping Nazis? These great world empires have all been reduced to footnotes in human history, because they all made a common mistake. They attacked the Jewish people, so God Almighty brought judgment upon them.

God promises to punish the nations that come against Israel

(Genesis 12:3). Every nation that comes against Israel, including the United States, is fighting not only against the people of Israel but also against God. God declares in His Word that He will judge all the nations of the world based on how they treat Israel and the Jewish people.

1 3
How Do the Four Blood Moons Relate to the Gog-Magog War?

The eclipse of the sun, such as the one that will occur on March 20, 2015—in the middle of the series of Four Blood Moons—is a sign of God's coming judgment on the nations. God is warning the world in the coming eclipse in the heavens. The eclipse that will be centered in the Tetrad of Four Blood Moons of 2014–25 is a clear signal that God is sending judgment on Gentile nations.

What will that coming judgment look like? The Bible refers to it as the Gog-Magog War, which will occur during the end times.

In Ezekiel 38, the prophet Ezekiel makes it very clear which nations are on God's hit list: Russia, Iran, Libya, Germany, Ethiopia, and Turkey.

Remember that an eclipse of the sun refers to Gentile nations. The message of the blood moon relates to Israel. So God's message to Israel, as He will reveal in the Four Blood Moons, is this: "As I delivered you from Pharaoh when you were in Egypt's bondage, I am going to deliver you from Russia, from Iran, from Turkey, from Libya, from Germany, from Ethiopia—from all of the nations who are saying, 'We are going to wipe you off the map.' I am going to deliver you as I delivered you from Haman's plot to exterminate you in ancient Persia. As I delivered you from Hitler's Holocaust. I will deliver you from Russia and Iran, who are talking about wiping you off the map. I am going to wipe Iran and Russia off the map." That's what God is saying through the coming Four Blood Moons. In this chapter, I'm going to prove that scripturally.

Through the Four Blood Moons of 2014–15, God is saying to Israel, "I am your Guardian. I am your Defender. I am your High Tower. I am your Shield."

The Jewish people are the apple of His eye. They are still cherished.

In Exodus 4:22, God says through Moses, "Israel is My son, My firstborn." What does that mean? Israel is the only nation created by a sovereign act of God. God is not going to let some empty-headed Iranian dictator crush what He has created and preserved all these thousands of years. Israel is going to prevail!

When is all of this going to happen? The prophet Joel tells us that these signs—the solar eclipse and blood moons described in Joel 2:30–31—will announce the destruction of those nations who join with Gog and Magog in attacking Jerusalem. This is the Gog-Magog War.

Joel then declares hope for all of Israel: "And it shall come to pass"—referring to the days of the Gog-Magog War—"that whoever calls on the name of the LORD shall be saved" (2:32). The literal Hebrew translation of "saved" in this verse means "physically spared."

Joel continues, "For in Mount Zion [Temple Mount] and in Jerusalem there shall be deliverance."

The fact is, the nation of Israel and those who turn to the God of Abraham, Isaac, and Jacob will be spared because the hand of God is going to preserve and defend Israel forever. Don't ever forget that.

The Gog-Magog War

In Ezekiel 38, the prophet Ezekiel gives a graphic and detailed description of the coming Gog-Magog War. As we look at this coming war and its possible connection with the Four Blood Moons, let's begin with today, where we are right now. How can we see the progression from right now to the Gog-Magog War?

Step 1: Israel, alone or assisted, will cripple Iran's nuclear capability.

Let me describe the "mission impossible" Israel is facing. Iran has about twelve different nuclear sites spread across the country. They are subterranean, buried in sixty feet of dirt, and then under that dirt there is a concrete encasement that houses those nuclear positions. Israel has a bunker bomb called a GB28 that will peel back ninety feet of dirt. But the trick will be to put another explosive device right in the crater of that bunker buster to crack the concrete. Every nuclear site the Iranians have is protected by the Russians' latest missile system. It is going to be "mission impossible." But Israel is going to get it done—*with* or *without* the help of America.

What is the result? When Israel attacks Iran's nuclear site, this attack will unify the rabidly anti-Israel Arab world, and they will join forces with Russia to invade Israel by land.

Step 2: Millions will march to war in an effort to overcome Israel.

Ezekiel goes on to describe the invading Russian-radical Islamic army as millions of people who will be marching to war in an effort to capture Jerusalem. The prophet says this army "will ascend, coming like a storm, covering the land like a cloud" (Ezekiel 38:9). That means as far as you can look—north, south, east, west—there will be an army of millions of people marching from these nations, coming to consume the nation of Israel. It will look to Israel and the world that Israel is hopelessly outnumbered and will be unable to survive.

STEP 3: GOD DECLARES WAR ON ISRAEL'S ENEMIES.

Then, in Ezekiel 38:2, God says to His prophet, "Son of man [Ezekiel], set your face against Gog [the man], of the land of Magog [his kingdom], the prince of Rosh [Russia], Meshech [Moscow], and Tubal [ancient city of Russia], and prophesy against him."

In other words, God tells Ezekiel to deliver a declaration of war against a *man* and *his kingdom*. If that were to happen today, the man would be Putin, and the kingdom would be Russia. That's how clear this prophecy is.

Who are the people mentioned in Ezekiel 38:2? How do we know who these people are?

Genesis 10:2 tells us that the sons of Japheth include Gomer, Magog, Tubal, and Meshech. Ethnologists (scientists who mark the migrations of nations) have traced the Japhethites from the Flood of Noah to Asia to the Black Sea and now to the land we call Russia.

God says, "You will come from your place out of the far north" (Ezekiel 38:15). If you take a map and draw a line straight north from Jerusalem (all directions in the Bible are given with regard to Jerusalem), it will go straight through Russia.

God declares war against these nations when he says to the

leader of this Russian-Iranian force, "Behold, I am against you" (Ezekiel 38:3). Now, when God Almighty declares war against you, you are going down. Remember, the sun's eclipse is a sign of God's judgment against the Gentile nations.

God continues, "I will turn you around, put hooks into your jaws, and lead you out" (Ezekiel 38:4). In other words, He is saying, "I'm going to drag you to the Middle East. I'm going to drag you to the hills of Israel." What is the "hook" God uses to bring these nations to Israel? The hook is *oil*. Russia has to have the oil for its military machinery—its trucks, its planes, its ships, and so forth. To be a military superpower, Russia will have to control the Persian Gulf oil, and it has to get Israel out of the way to have that control. That's the hook.

THE NATIONS OF THE GOG-MAGOG WAR

In Ezekiel 38:5, God puts together his hit list of the nations He is going to destroy when they invade Israel: "Persia, Ethiopia, and Libya are with them, all of them with shield and helmet; Gomer and all its troops; the house of Togarmah from the far north and all its troops—many people are with you."

PERSIA

The first nation on God's hit list is *Persia*. Persia is modern-day Iran. I want to say this clearly: sins you don't confess, God does not forgive and He does not forget. He has a very long memory. Haman's plot to exterminate the Jews in ancient Persia is still on God's books. Now we have a Persian leader in Iran, Ahmadinejad, saying he is going to wipe Israel off the map? Wrong! There's a Spy in the sky and He's Jewish and He's watching out for the benefit of Israel.

ETHIOPIA

Then Ezekiel lists *Ethiopia*. This refers to the Ethiopia of the Bible, not necessarily the modern country of Ethiopia as we know it today.

LIBYA

The third nation is *Libya*, where our US ambassador and three US Marines were recently murdered by an Islamic mob. Listen to me: it was not the result of a cheap movie, as we are currently being told by our State Department. Americans know better and we deserve the truth about the murder of our ambassador and those three good marines who laid their lives down!

GERMANY

The next nation is *Germany*. "Gomer" is Germany. People don't make the connection between Germany and the Islamic nations. Let me tell you about a story that recently appeared in the *Jerusalem Post*. Germany is Iran's number-one trading partner. Recently a group of German business leaders went to Iran, over the protests of the Jewish community of Germany, to plan for the future. Think of it: Germany, the nation who put together the Holocaust, is going to do business with Iran, the nation who denies that the Holocaust ever happened! The news says that Germany spends four billion euros per year with Iran. God is sitting in heaven with His logbook, saying, "There is going to be a payday someday, and I have not forgotten the Holocaust. I am going to bring you to the hills of Israel, and when you get here I'm going to settle my account on behalf of my children, Israel." That's going to happen!

RUSSIA

The leader of the invading armies is *Russia*. Look at Ezekiel 38:7. God labels the Russians as a leader: "Prepare yourself and be ready, you and all your companies that are gathered about you; and be a guard for them." He tells Russia to be a guard to the invading armies. The word *guard* means "commander." God is telling Russia, be a commander unto them.

This scripture suggests that America has lost its superpower status, and Russia and Iran are not afraid to invade Israel as America watches without responding. Look at Ezekiel 38:10: "On that day [the day you invade the land] it will come to pass that thoughts will arise in your mind [the invading force], and you shall make an evil plan." What is that evil plan? To capture Jerusalem!

God continues, "You [Russia, Iran, and those who come with them] will say, 'I will go up against a land of unwalled villages'" (v. 11).

What does "unwalled villages" mean? Here Ezekiel is portraying Jerusalem as being without protection. Why? Because in the Old Testament the wall around your city represented your military defense system. Babylon had a wall so wide you could race four chariots around its top. If you had an insignificant wall, you had a very weak military system. Ezekiel is describing Israel as having no walls—no protection at all! The point here isn't the walls; it's the symbolism of protection. Israel has no protection.

When Israel was reborn in 1948, President Harry Truman recognized the State of Israel in eleven minutes. He declared it with the full force and might of the American military. And make no mistake: in 1948 we were a superpower. We had just defeated the Nazis and the Axis power, our dollar had been proclaimed as the absolute supreme currency, and hands down we were number one, respected, and feared around the world. But today America is war weary, and we have a right to be war weary.

Israel is without the protection of the West. The enemies of Israel smell our weakness and our lack of willingness to respond. When a US ambassador and three marines are murdered and we don't respond, that means the green light is signaling for them to do what they want. The enemies of Israel are smelling the weakness of the West.

GOD FIGHTS FOR ISRAEL

What happens next? The prophet Ezekiel tells us:

> Sheba [Yemen], Dedan [Saudi Arabia], the merchants of Tarshish [Great Britain], and all their young lions [including America, because we came out of Great Britain] will say to you, "Have you come to take plunder? Have you gathered your army to take booty, to carry away silver and gold, to take away livestock and goods, to take great plunder?"

> —EZEKIEL 38:13

Think about it: all these countries will look at this massive Russian-Iranian military monster machine and ask, "Have you come to take plunder?" If you could take an Academy Award for the most supremely stupid question ever asked, this would be the winner, hands down.

Right here in the book of Ezekiel, chapter 38, God loses His cool. His anger and His wrath explode. After centuries of watching nations abuse the Jewish people, after centuries of watching the pogroms in Russia, the Holocaust in Germany, and the abuse and anti-Semitism in Europe, God's righteous anger turns loose.

> "And it will come to pass at the same time, when Gog comes against the land of Israel," says the Lord GOD, "that My fury will show in My face."
>
> —EZEKIEL 38:18

God Almighty is going to go to war for Israel. God, who is merciful and mighty, says, "Enough! I am furious with the enemies of Israel."

He says, "I will turn thee back, and leave but the sixth part of thee" (Ezekiel 39:2 KJV). The King James Version is the nearest version to the original Hebrew text. God says He will leave only a sixth of the invading army. In other words, God is going to kill 84 percent of the Russian-Arab force. The king of Russia will be killed. The king of the Islamic force will be defeated by the hand of God. God says it's *over* for them!

How will God destroy this army of millions of people? He gives the story in Ezekiel 38:19.

EARTHQUAKE

The first thing that is going to happen is an earthquake. God is going to cause an earthquake to swallow a significant part of that army.

You say, "God would never do that!" Well, you are mistaken: God has already done that.

Remember when the nation of Israel was having a little administrative problem? Numbers 16 tells the story. Some of the people didn't like Moses and were grumbling against him. So God basically said to Moses, "Tell all the people who are speaking against you to come to the tent of meeting. We're going to have a departmental meeting now."

God opened the ground, swallowed them all, and buried them alive. Problem solved: Moses was the leader. That's power.

FRIENDLY FIRE

The second way God is going to attack this invading army is with what we call today "friendly fire." The Bible calls it, "Every man's sword will be against his brother" (Ezekiel 38:21). Think about it: there are nine invading armies, speaking different languages, using different military methods and weapons—ideal circumstances for chaos and confusion.

You say, "Well, that could never happen." But it already happened!

Do you remember when Gideon blew the trumpets and broke the pitchers? The enemies of Israel were so confused that they fought each other. Israel won the victory and they never pulled a sword (Judges 7).

God is going to do it again! God's not doing anything new; He's just pulling out old tricks to play on new enemies.

HAILSTONES

The third thing God is going to do, according to Ezekiel 38:22, is send hailstones. Look at it: "I will rain down on him, on his troops, and on the many peoples who are with him, flooding rain, great hailstones, fire, and brimstone." Now the text suggests that these hailstones weigh one hundred pounds. They're big. Why? Because in the Old Testament, sinners were stoned. (Thank God they don't do that anymore!) But God Himself is going to stone the invading armies.

You say, "God wouldn't do that!" That's wrong. God has already done that.

Joshua 10:11 records the outcome of five armies attacking Israel. They were going to destroy Israel. The Bible says: "The LORD cast down large hailstones from heaven on them [the enemies of Israel] . . . and they died. There were more who died from the hailstones than children of Israel killed with the sword." The message? Don't tick God off! When He turns loose, you're not going to win!

RESULT OF GOG-MAGOG WAR

In Ezekiel 39:7, God tells us why He is doing this: "I will make My holy name known in the midst of My people Israel, and I will not let them profane My holy name anymore." God says He will take these actions against Israel's enemies for this reason: so the Jewish people will know beyond a shadow of a doubt that *God* is their refuge, not Washington!

The verse continues, "Then the nations [that's us, the Gentiles] shall know that I am the LORD, the Holy One in Israel." All of the atheists and all of the agnostics will not be able to explain how Israel was delivered from this massive army. Not since God destroyed Pharaoh and his Egyptian army has God wiped out an army like he's going to wipe out Russia and Iran. It will take Israel seven months to bury the dead and seven years to burn the weapons of war.

GOD'S PLAN FOR ISRAEL'S FUTURE

Look at God's message to the Jewish people in the closing stanza of Ezekiel 39: "So the house of Israel shall know that I am the LORD their God from that day forward" (v. 22). He continues, "I will bring back the captives of Jacob, and have mercy on the whole house of Israel; and I will be jealous for My holy name" (v. 25).

What is the future for Israel? Mercy! What is God's plan for Israel? Deliverance! Israel, you are not alone. The God of Abraham, Isaac, and Jacob is with you!

> "I will not hide My face from them anymore; for I shall have poured out My Spirit on the house of Israel," says the Lord GOD.
>
> —EZEKIEL 39:29

Why is this message important to our Jewish friends? Because the Holy One of Israel has sworn to defend Israel. When the Jewish people see this battle approaching, God is essentially saying to them, "Do not fear. Washington may not be with you. But the God of Abraham, Isaac, and Jacob is with you. You are still the apple of God's eye. You are still the chosen people. As God delivered you from Pharaoh . . . as He delivered you from Haman's plot . . . as He delivered you from the British white-paper policy, God will deliver you again. Your greatest victory, O house of Israel, is right in front of you because the God of Abraham, Isaac, and Jacob is alive and well and He is going to fight for your defense!"

POSSIBLE CONNECTION WITH THE FOUR BLOOD MOONS?

When is this going to happen? Jewish scholars say Joel 2:30–31 (the biblical passage where the blood moons appear) is in the context of the Gog-Magog War. NASA says the Four Blood Moons will occur between April 2014 and September 2015.

Why is this message so important to Christians? Consider the scenario for the future. Iran is going to become nuclear, sooner or later. When Israel hits Iran's nuclear centers, this action is going to unite Russia, Iran, Germany, Libya, Ethiopia, and the enemies of Israel to retaliate and to invade the land of Israel, according to Ezekiel.

We see this already beginning to happen right now on the news on our televisions every night. We see the rage and the unity of Islamic nations against Israel and America. We are seeing the first stages of the Gog-Magog War. In the future, the Russian-led coalition of radical Islamic armies will march on Israel—and the moment their feet touch Israel's soil, God is going annihilate that army.

The Jewish people will be reconciled to the God of Abraham,

Isaac, and Jacob, according to Ezekiel 39:22 and 39:25–29. All the righteous Jews of the world will return to Israel, and God will pour out His Spirit on the house of Israel.

This display of God's power will serve as a final warning to the world that we are living in the final second of the dispensation of grace. Churches everywhere who understand the first element of Bible prophecy will be packed with people anticipating the coming of the Lord Jesus Christ.

The nations of Gog and Magog are uniting right now. The message of the Four Blood Moons is this: God is going to defend Israel in His time. He is going to destroy the nations that invade Israel, and Jesus Christ the Son of God could come at any second, right now.

The King is coming!

Will the Second Coming Happen in Our Lifetime?

Are we currently living in the generation who will see the physical and glorious return of our Lord Jesus Christ? Will the Second Coming happen in our lifetime?

In *Four Blood Moons*, we looked at Jesus' Prophecy Conference on the Mount of Olives in detail and discovered that Jesus gave several signs that would indicate the coming of the end of the age and His return. We also studied many other biblical prophecies related to the Second Coming of Christ.

After deeply studying the many prophetic passages of the Bible for more than fifty-four years and carefully watching for the biblical signs of the end times, I have come to the conclusion that we are, indeed, living in the terminal generation. In this chapter, I will show you twelve prophetic signs that, I believe, clearly indicate that the Second Coming of Christ will happen in our lifetime.

1. Rebirth of Israel (Isaiah 66:8–10)
2. The Ingathering (Jeremiah 23:7–8)
3. Jewish control of Jerusalem (Luke 21:24)
4. Deception on a global scale (Matthew 24:4–5)
5. The resurrection of the Hebrew language (Zephaniah 3:9)
6. The knowledge explosion (Daniel 12:4)
7. The birth of nuclear warfare (Zechariah 14:12–15)
8. Famines, pestilences, and earthquakes (Matthew 24:7–8)

9. Anarchy (Matthew 24:12)
10. "As the days of Noah were . . ." (Matthew 24:36–39)
11. International instant communication (Revelation 11:3, 7–10)
12. Worldwide evangelism (Matthew 24:14)

I covered the first nine of these prophetic signs in *Four Blood Moons*. I'll briefly review them here and then discuss the final three signs.

Rebirth of Israel

Who has heard such a thing?
Who has seen such things?
Shall the earth be made to give birth in one day?
Or shall a nation be born at once?
For as soon as Zion was in labor,
She gave birth to her children.

—Isaiah 66:8

I remember very clearly the day of May 15, 1948, when I was sitting at the kitchen table with my father, a quiet man with a brilliant mind. I was eight years old, and we were listening to the evening news on the radio.

The radio crackled as the reporter made anannouncement that brought tears to my father's eyes: "The United Nations has today announced that they have formally recognized the State of Israel."

My father put down the book he had been holding and was silent for a moment. Then he looked me in the eyes and said, "We have just heard the most important prophetic message that will ever be delivered until Jesus Christ returns to earth. This is the greatest miracle of the twentieth century."

As I have studied the Bible and specifically its prophecies concerning the end times and Israel, I have discovered that my father was exactly right. Biblical prophecy is clear that the nation of Israel must be reborn before Messiah comes.

When the disciples came to Jesus and asked Him for a sign of the end of the age, He responded with the parable of the fig tree:

Now learn this parable from the fig tree: When its branch has already become tender and puts forth leaves, you know that summer is near. So you also, when you see all these things, know that it is near—at the doors! Assuredly, I say to you, this generation will by no means pass away till all these things take place.

—MATTHEW 24:32–34

In biblical prophecy, Israel is often pictured as a fig tree. This parable reveals that "when its branch has already become tender and puts forth leaves," then the time of Jesus' return is near. The rebirth of Israel, sprouting new leaves on the fig tree as the Jews return to their homeland, is one of the most obvious prophetic signs that we are living in the end times. The generation that sees the rebirth of Israel is the terminal generation.

The Ingathering

> "Therefore, behold, the days are coming," says the LORD, "that they shall no longer say, 'As the LORD lives who brought up the children of Israel from the land of Egypt,' but, 'As the LORD lives who brought up and led the descendants of the house of Israel from the north country and from all the countries where I had driven them.' And they shall dwell in their own land."
>
> —JEREMIAH 23:7–8

Another sign that we are in living in the terminal generation is the Ingathering—or the Jews returning home to the land of Israel.

In AD 70, the Roman general Titus invaded Jerusalem, demolished the Temple, and destroyed the city. The citizens of Israel fled for their lives in an event that would become known as the Diaspora —or scattering of the Jews into the nations throughout the world. For two thousand years, the Jewish people were without a homeland to call their own.

Then on May 15, 1948, the State of Israel was reborn. The Israeli Declaration of Independence says, "The State of Israel is open to Jewish immigration and the Ingathering of Exiles." The Law of Return, enacted on July 5, 1950, extends to every Jew on the earth the right to immigrate to Israel.

The Ingathering continues to this day, as Jews from all over the world continue to return to their homeland. Thousands of Jews now dwell there and are raising up the first new generation of Jewish people whose roots are plunged deep into Israeli soil.

JEWISH CONTROL OF JERUSALEM

Jerusalem will be trampled by Gentiles until the times of the Gentiles are fulfilled.

—LUKE 21:24

Another sign that we are living in the terminal generation is that Jerusalem is no longer under Gentile control. Jesus told His disciples that someday "the times of the Gentiles" would be "fulfilled" (Luke 21:24). After that time, the Bible says, the Lord will rebuild Zion (Jerusalem) and appear there in His glory (Psalm 102:16).

As we saw in our study of *Four Blood Moons*, this sign was fulfilled as a result of the miraculous Six-Day War. On June 7, 1967, Israel's troops retook the Temple Mount against unbelievable odds. For the first time since AD 70, the Jewish people finally regained control of Jerusalem, the everlasting capital of Israel and the city of God.

DECEPTION ON A GLOBAL SCALE

Jesus answered and said to them: "Take heed that no one deceives you. For many will come in My name, saying, 'I am the Christ,' and will deceive many."

—MATTHEW 24:4–5

Another biblical indicator that we are living in the terminal generation is the prevalence of deception all over the world. Although there has always been deception in the world, in recent years, lying has been elevated to an art form.

Truth is no longer simply stated—it's spun, manipulated, glossed over, and adjusted to fit whatever a person desires. We have become so accustomed to telling and believing lies in our homes, in our communities, our schools, our courts, our congress, and even in the White House!

Our society teaches that there is no such thing as absolute right and wrong. Environmentalists take extreme measures to protect "Mother Earth." Our politicians keep spending money they don't have, believing we can somehow repay our debts. And in all areas of life, the Bible is mocked and its followers made to look like buffoons by the media.

We are clearly living in the days spoken of by the prophet Jeremiah: "Everyone will deceive his neighbor, and will not speak the truth; they have taught their tongue to speak lies; they weary themselves to commit iniquity" (Jeremiah 9:5).

THE RESURRECTION OF THE HEBREW LANGUAGE

For then I will restore to the peoples a pure language,
That they all may call on the name of the LORD,
To serve Him with one accord.

—ZEPHANIAH 3:9

The Bible says that before the Second Coming of Christ, God will restore to His people a "pure language"—the Hebrew language.

After the Roman siege of AD 70, the Jews fled from their homeland and were scattered around the nations of the world. As they settled into their new lives in these foreign countries, the

Jews began speaking the languages of the countries in which they were living. The Hebrew language was used only for studying the Scriptures. With each passing generation, the spoken language of Hebrew began to disappear.

Until one Jew decided it was time to bring it back.

Eliezer Ben-Yehuda was a newspaper editor and Jewish nationalist who came to Jerusalem in 1881. He wanted to unite the Jewish people from all over the world—and he decided the best way to do that would be through a common spoken language. He made it his life's mission to make Hebrew the modern language of the Jewish people. One month before he died, the British authorities declared Hebrew to be the official language of the Jews, fulfilling this Bible prophecy.

THE KNOWLEDGE EXPLOSION

But as for you, Daniel, conceal these words and seal up the book until the end of time; many will go back and forth, and knowledge will increase.

—DANIEL 12:4 NASB

In the last few years, we have experienced a knowledge explosion like the world has never seen. Until the twentieth century, life was relatively the same in terms of technology. People walked or rode horses. They wrote with pens on paper. If they wanted to talk to someone, they had to arrange to meet him or her in person.

Just think how much has changed in just one generation! In the span of only a few years, mankind invented cars, planes, and the space shuttle. We saw the invention of the telegraph, telephone, fax machine, and cell phone. We now watch movies and television shows on high-definition, flat-screen TVs. We store hundreds of books on a single electronic device. Medical advances have drastically improved our quality of life and increased our average life span by several years. We can use our smartphones—small enough to fit in our pockets—to talk to anyone in the world, have constant connection with people via e-mail and social media, and log on to the Internet to access the vast data available to us on the information superhighway.

Today's technology is advancing so quickly that whatever device you purchase is obsolete by the time you walk out of the store! But has this rapid increase of knowledge produced wisdom?

In 2 Timothy 3, the apostle Paul says that in the latter days, people will be "always learning and never able to come to the knowledge of the truth" (v. 7). No matter how advanced our technology and how vast our access to limitless information, we cannot find truth or wisdom apart from God and His Word.

THE BIRTH OF NUCLEAR WARFARE

And this shall be the plague with which the Lord will strike all the people who fought against Jerusalem:

Their flesh shall dissolve while they stand on their feet,
Their eyes shall dissolve in their sockets,
And their tongues shall dissolve in their mouths.
It shall come to pass in that day

That a great panic from the LORD will be among them.

Everyone will seize the hand of his neighbor,

And raise his hand against his neighbor's hand;

Judah also will fight at Jerusalem.

And the wealth of all the surrounding nations

Shall be gathered together:

Gold, silver, and apparel in great abundance.

Such also shall be the plague

On the horse and the mule,

On the camel and the donkey,

And on all the cattle that will be in those camps.

So shall this plague be.

—ZECHARIAH 14:12–15

As recently as my father's generation, there were certain prophetic passages of Scripture that even Bible scholars simply couldn't understand. One such incomprehensible passage is Zechariah 14:12–15, which describes a devastating plague in the Middle East unlike anything the earth has ever seen.

How could people's flesh dissolve while they were still standing? How could their eyes and tongues literally melt away? For centuries, mankind could not comprehend what could cause such a horror.

Then in 1939, the Manhattan Project was born, ushering in the nuclear age with the invention of the atomic bomb. Next came the hydrogen bomb, which could in a fraction of a second produce 1.5 billion degrees of heat—such an intense degree that a person's flesh could actually fall off his body before the corpse hits the ground. A blast from one of today's one-megaton bombs would instantly atomize anything within a two-mile radius. Within an eight-mile radius, everything would be set on fire, igniting the surrounding area as a raging inferno.

In Revelation 9:15, John tells us that four angels will be released to destroy one-third of the earth's population in a single day. Before nuclear warfare, this was impossible. But now the world has enough nuclear weaponry to kill every person on earth twenty times over. It's only a matter of time before the instability of the Middle East, inflamed by radical Islamic terrorists, results in nuclear warfare— and I believe it will happen sometime in our generation.

FAMINES, PESTILENCES, AND EARTHQUAKES

For nation will rise against nation, and kingdom against kingdom. And there will be famines, pestilences, and earth-quakes in various places. All these are the beginning of sorrows.

—MATTHEW 24:7–8

Jesus told His disciples that they could know the time of the end of the age was drawing near when they observed a rise of famines, pestilences, and earthquakes around the world. We discussed this at length in chapter 9 of *Four Blood Moons*.

The United States of America produces enough food to feed the entire world, yet we subsidize farmers not to grow certain crops or exceed a certain limit lest the overages drive down the market price.

A large percentage of frustrated American farmers have abandoned agricultural life in favor of urban careers, leaving no one behind to care for the family farm. As our farms lie dormant, approximately one in seven American families is unsure where their next meal will come from. Meanwhile, millions of people around the world are dying of starvation. The time is drawing near when the world, *including America*, will no longer be able to produce enough food to feed our massive global population.

People are dying not only of starvation, but they are dying from "pestilences," or pandemic diseases that spread faster than our ability to vaccinate or treat. Recent years have seen a sharp rise in killer viruses, including AIDS, SARS, swine flu, and the H7N3 bird flu virus, in addition to antibiotic-resistant bacteria.

Jesus also told His disciples to watch for "earthquakes" before His coming. In the Bible, God repeatedly used earthquakes to get the attention of people and achieve His divine purposes. God announced the giving of the Law with an earthquake (Exodus 19:18), He used an earthquake to swallow those who opposed His plan (Numbers 16:31–33), and He sent an earthquake to shake loose the prison chains of Paul and Silas (Acts 16:25–28). God sent an earthquake at the crucifixion to tear the veil in the Temple from top to bottom, opening direct access to the presence of God for every believer (Matthew 27:51). Then He sent another earthquake on resurrection morning to roll away the stone from the tomb—not to let Jesus out, but to let us in (Matthew 28:2).

Seismologists and geologists have become increasingly aware of and able to measure the almost constant trembling of the earth, and they are now forecasting that "the Big One" is coming. Some experts think this earthquake could split America in half. But that's nothing compared to the really "Big One" that's coming, according to the Bible! Revelation 16:18–20 describes "a great earthquake, such a mighty and great earthquake as had not occurred since men were on the earth." God is shaking things up on planet earth as a sign to us that we are living in the terminal generation.

ANARCHY

> Because lawlessness will abound, the love of many will grow cold.
>
> —MATTHEW 24:12

In His Olivet Discourse, Jesus revealed that before He returns the nations of the world will descend into a state of lawlessness and anarchy. We discussed this dismal condition in chapter 9 of *Four Blood Moons.*

We are seeing the fulfillment of this prophecy every single day on our televisions and in our streets. From the Occupy Wall Street mobs of Union Square in New York to angry protestors rioting and screaming obscenities, America is no longer "one nation under God"—or under any authority, for that matter. Instead, we have become millions of separate individuals, each person fervently looking out for his or her own interests and having no regard for what is best for our entire nation.

Like the Jewish people who had no national leadership during the days of the judges, Americans—and the world—today could be accurately described in these words: "Everyone did what was right in his own eyes" (Judges 21:25). However people may justify their self-serving, lawless behavior—and by whatever name they call it—it's anarchy!

"As the Days of Noah Were . . ."

> But as the days of Noah were, so also will the coming of the Son of Man be. For as in the days before the flood, they were eating and drinking, marrying and giving in marriage, until the day that Noah entered the ark, and did not know until the flood came and took them all away, so also will the coming of the Son of Man be.
>
> —Matthew 24:37–39

Jesus told His disciples that the days of His return would be "as the days of Noah were." What was life like during the "days of Noah"? The Bible tells us that it was a time of great depravity and perversion. "The wickedness of man was great in the earth, and . . . every intent of the thoughts of his heart was only evil continually" (Genesis 6:5).

These very words could be written about our generation today! America has plummeted into the cesspool of immorality, with popular television shows and movies glorifying sexual perversions and "alternative" lifestyles. Promiscuity is at an all-time high as young people brag about being "open" and "tolerant." But this so-called tolerance hasn't led to freedom; it has only resulted in an increase in abuse, incest, sexually transmitted disease, and the collapse of the traditional family.

During the days leading up to the Flood, the people watched and laughed at Noah as he built the ark. For one hundred twenty years, they continually mocked Noah while they reveled in their wickedness, partied, ate and drank, and completely ignored the message of coming doom.

And then one day, suddenly, the skies darkened and the first raindrop fell. The people had ignored Noah's warnings, and now there was no escape from God's judgment on the earth—He had already shut the door of the ark to snatch away Noah and his family, keeping them safe from the coming storm.

Prophetically speaking, believers today are in the same position as Noah when he had built the ark. The message has been preached, and those who believe are getting onboard with Christ. We know that one day, suddenly, the trump will sound as Jesus comes to rapture the church away from His coming judgment on the earth.

INTERNATIONAL INSTANT COMMUNICATION

I will give power to my two witnesses, and they will prophesy one thousand two hundred and sixty days, clothed in sackcloth. . . . When they finish their testimony, the beast that ascends out of the bottomless pit will make war against them, overcome them, and kill them. And their dead bodies will lie in the street of the great city which spiritually is called Sodom and Egypt, where also our Lord was crucified. Then those from the peoples, tribes, tongues, and nations will see their dead bodies three-and-a-half days, and not allow their dead bodies to be put into graves. And those who dwell on the earth will rejoice over them, make merry, and send gifts to one another, because these two prophets tormented those who dwell on the earth.

—REVELATION 11:3, 7–10

In the book of Revelation, the apostle John tells of the two witnesses who will appear on the earth during the Great Tribulation. These witnesses call upon men to repent of their sins and turn to God.

For centuries, people could not comprehend how "the peoples, tribes, tongues, and nations"—the entire world—could see the two witnesses at the same time. How could people in different countries and on different continents all be watching the same scene? How could the testimony of the two witnesses reach the entire world?

Then came television, followed by international satellites, the Internet, and now wireless communication where you can stream live events on the screen of your smartphone. This was not possible in my father's generation! But it *is* possible today, because we are living in the terminal generation.

WORLDWIDE EVANGELISM

And this gospel of the kingdom will be preached in all the world as a witness to all the nations, and then the end will come.

—MATTHEW 24:14

Jesus said that the gospel would be preached to the entire world before the end would come. We looked at the "gospel of the kingdom" in detail in chapter 10 of *Four Blood Moons*. Here I want to point out the extent to which this gospel will be preached.

Never before in the history of the world has it been possible for a single message to be communicated to every tribe, tongue, nation, and people group in the world. The task was simply too monumental, even for the most dedicated missionaries going to the remotest places.

But today's technology has opened the door to this possibility. Christian broadcasters are reaching millions of places through television, radio, and Internet broadcasts. Bibles are being made available for every people group in the world to read and hear the message of the gospel in their native language. And the *JESUS* film—a two-hour docudrama on the life of Christ—has been shown in every country of the world in hundreds of languages.

The gospel is encircling the entire globe as a witness to all the nations on earth, just as Jesus said it would! Look up and observe the prophecies being fulfilled before our very eyes. We are the terminal generation!

15

How Do the Jewish Feasts Relate to the End Times?

The seven Jewish feasts, given by God to His people in the Holy Scriptures, are God's blueprint for the future. These feasts are not just for the Jewish people. The Bible says these are *the feasts of the Lord,* which means that if you are with the Lord—whether Jew or Gentile—these feasts are for you. I assure you that when Jesus returns we're going to keep these feasts. The message and mystery of these feasts are for every generation. The Jewish feasts reveal the seven most important themes of the Bible.

The word "feast" in Hebrew is *mo'ed,* and it means "a set time." It's an appointed time, something done exactly at a certain time. David refers to this in Psalm 102:13 when he says, "You will arise and have mercy on Zion [Israel]; for the time to favor her, yes, the *set time,* has come." The God we serve is running the universe with exact, stopwatch time. Nothing is happenstance; it is all ordained of God. If you do not understand the prophetic significance of the feasts of the Lord, it's like breaking the hands off your clock—how will you be able to tell the *set time*?

Another word connected with Hebrew feasts is *mikrah,* meaning "a rehearsal or recital." Each of these seven events is a recital for something that is going to happen in our future. It's a rehearsal so that you can see it. Keep in mind when God gave these seven feasts in Leviticus 23, He was communicating with a people who, for the most part, could not read. So He taught them His principles through the drama of the feasts with a point of reference that they all could grasp. He gave them seven feasts to guide them through the centuries between the giving of the Law at Sinai and the return and reign of Messiah the King.

The seven Jewish feasts are a spiritual blueprint revealing what lies ahead for Jerusalem, Israel, and the rest of the world. In this chapter, we will look at each of these seven feasts to discover its connection to Israel, biblical prophecy, and the end times.

THE FEASTS OF THE LORD

In Leviticus 23, God outlined seven major feasts to be celebrated every year by the Jewish people:

1. The Feast of Passover—*Pesach*
2. The Feast of Unleavened Bread
3. The Feast of Firstfruits
4. The Feast of Pentecost—*Shavuot*
5. The Feast of Trumpets—*Rosh Hashanah*
6. The Feast of Atonement—*Yom Kippur*
7. The Feast of Tabernacles—*Sukkot*

The first three feasts (the spring feasts) were fulfilled in Jesus' first coming. The fourth feast was fulfilled fifty days after He ascended into heaven, on the Day of Pentecost, the birthday of the church. I'll briefly review these four feasts before we move on to the final three feasts (the fall feasts), which testify of Christ's Second Coming.

THE FEASTS OF CHRIST'S FIRST COMING

THE FEAST OF PASSOVER—*PESACH*

We examined the prophetic significance of the Feast of Passover on pages 176–79 of *Four Blood Moons*. There, we learned that the Feast of Passover is a time of redemption. Passover begins on the fifteenth day of the Jewish month of Nissan, which is between March and April in our Western calendars.

The word *Pesach* comes from the Hebrew word meaning to "pass over," which refers to the fact that God "passed over" the houses of the Jewish people who applied the blood of the Passover lamb to the doorposts of their homes. *Pesach* is also the name of the sacrificial lamb offered in the Temple on this holiday.

Jesus Christ fulfilled the prophecy of Passover at the cross. He was crucified during the Feast of Passover. John says He is the "Lamb of God who takes away the sin of the world" (John 1:29). Peter says He is God's lamb, without spot or blemish, sacrificed for us (1 Peter 1:19). The apostle Paul said that "Christ, our Passover, was sacrificed for us" (1 Corinthians 5:7).

THE FEAST OF UNLEAVENED BREAD

The Feast of Unleavened Bread takes place immediately after the sacrifice of the Passover lamb. It is recorded in Exodus 12:14–16:

> So this day shall be to you a memorial; and you shall keep it as a feast to the LORD throughout your generations. You shall keep it as a feast by an everlasting ordinance. Seven days you shall eat unleavened bread. On the first day you

shall remove leaven from your houses. For whoever eats leavened bread from the first day until the seventh day, that person shall be cut off from Israel. On the first day there shall be a holy convocation, and on the seventh day there shall be a holy convocation for you. No manner of work shall be done on them; but that which everyone must eat—that only may be prepared by you.

The Feast of Unleavened Bread lasts for seven days. During these seven days, the Jewish people were forbidden to eat any leaven (yeast). Why? Throughout the Bible, *leaven* is a metaphor for sin. It represents the pride and arrogance that lead people to think they have no need of God. Jesus said, "Take heed and beware of the leaven of the Pharisees and the Sadducees" (Matthew 16:6). The apostle Paul pointed out the devastating, widespread effect that even a "little" pride can have on our lives: "Your glorying is not good. Do you not know that a little leaven leavens the whole lump?" (1 Corinthians 5:6).

Just as the matzo of the Feast of the Unleavened Bread is without leaven, Jesus Christ came and lived a sinless life, and He is seated at the right hand of the Father in heaven, a sinless Savior for you and for me. The message of the Feast of Unleavened Bread is that redemption is to be followed by a holy life and right living.

THE FEAST OF FIRSTFRUITS

The term *firstfruits* refers to the first portion of the harvest. God told His people to set aside the very first fruits of each harvest season as an offering to Him.

Speak to the children of Israel, and say to them: "When you come into the land which I give to you, and reap its harvest, then you shall bring a sheaf of the *firstfruits* of your harvest to the priest."

—LEVITICUS 23:10

The firstfruits were a pledge of the harvest to follow, and offering them to God was a way of expressing trust in God's provision—that just as He provided the firstfruits, He would provide the rest of the harvest for His people.

The Feast of Firstfruits commemorates resurrection, for God took an enslaved, spiritually dead people and gave them new life. It represents the resurrection of Jesus Christ, who rose from the dead to demonstrate His power over death, hell, and sin. This feast not only foreshadows the resurrection of Jesus Christ, but it also foreshadows the resurrection of every believer! When the apostle Paul explained the resurrection of believers, he referred to Christ as "our firstfruits": "For as in Adam all die, even so in Christ all shall be made alive. But each one in his own order: *Christ the firstfruits*, afterward those who are Christ's at His coming" (1 Corinthians 15:22–23).

Like Jesus Christ our firstfruits, someday we, too, will be given glorious new, resurrection bodies!

THE FEAST OF PENTECOST—*SHAVUOT*

Fifty days after the Feast of Firstfruits comes the Feast of the Pentecost. Sometimes referred to as *Shavuot* ("Weeks"), this feast is a celebration of thanksgiving for the completed grain harvest.

> Count fifty days to the day after the seventh Sabbath; then
> you shall offer a new grain offering to the LORD. . . . And
> you shall proclaim on the same day that it is a holy con-
> vocation to you. You shall do no customary work on it. It
> shall be a statute forever in all your dwellings throughout
> your generations.
>
> —LEVITICUS 23:16, 21

When the nation of Israel brought forth the abundant grain God
provided them in the Promised Land at the end of the harvest, it
was a time of great rejoicing! This celebration is a reminder that
every good and perfect gift comes from Him.

Fifty days after Christ's resurrection (the fulfillment of Firstfruits) came the Day of Pentecost. On that day. God fulfilled the
Feast of Pentecost by giving His people a "good and perfect gift"
that was greater than they could ever imagine! Acts 2:1–4 tells
the story:

> When the Day of Pentecost had fully come, they were all
> with one accord in one place. And suddenly there came a
> sound from heaven, as of a rushing mighty wind, and it
> filled the whole house where they were sitting. Then there
> appeared to them divided tongues, as of fire, and one sat
> upon each of them. And they were all filled with the Holy
> Spirit and began to speak with other tongues, as the Spirit
> gave them utterance.

God does not simply want to dwell *with* us; He wants to dwell *in* us! On the Day of Pentecost, He sent His Holy Spirit to come and dwell *in* His people. In 1 Corinthians 6:19, we are told: "your body is the temple of *the Holy Spirit who is in you*, whom you have from God, and you are not your own."

Why is the fulfillment of Pentecost—the giving of the Holy Spirit—so important? When the Holy Spirit is in you, you have power over the flesh and the devil. When the Holy Spirit is in you, you have power over sickness. You have power over disease. You have power over demon spirits. You have power over fear. When the Holy Spirit is in you, you have power over doubt and insecurity. When the Holy Spirit is in you, you can ask and God will give it because you are the anointed of God.

With the Holy Spirit living in you, you have supernatural power. You have the gift of faith to believe for the impossible—it may not be possible with you, but it is possible with God. You have the gift of healing. With the Holy Spirit you have the gift of miracles, where God breaks or accelerates the laws of nature to help you accomplish the mission He has given you.

When you have the Holy Spirit in you, you have the power to speak with authority and clarity over your future for the purposes of God!

THE FEASTS OF CHRIST'S SECOND COMING

So far we have briefly observed how Jesus Christ and the coming of the Holy Spirit has fulfilled the first four of the feasts of the Lord. Now let's examine in more detail the final three feasts of the Lord, the prophetic feasts that are awaiting fulfillment in the coming end-times events of the Rapture, the Second Coming, and the millennial kingdom.

THE FEAST OF TRUMPETS—ROSH HASHANAH
(Future Fulfillment: The Rapture)

The first feast prophecy yet to be fulfilled is the Feast of Trumpets, or Rosh Hashanah. The Feast of Trumpets happens in our month of September.

> Speak to the children of Israel, saying: "In the seventh month, on the first day of the month, you shall have a sabbath-rest, a memorial of blowing of trumpets, a holy convocation. You shall do no customary work on it; and you shall offer an offering made by fire to the LORD."
>
> —LEVITICUS 23:24–25

The trumpet used in the feast is the shofar. It's not a silver trumpet like you see nowadays; it's a ram's horn. The shofar is the trumpet used to announce the beginning of the feast. It was used to assemble the people.

Think about it: how do you move two million people across the wilderness? You have a group of people who are blowing horns, and those horns are signals for the people. And by the particular way they blow that horn—by the long blast or short blast, something like a Morse code of sound—the people of Israel knew whether to pack up and move out or sit down where they were. The trumpet blast was their form of communicating with a large group of people.

The sound of the shofar announced the year of Jubilee, the year of the release of all debts. The shofar was also used to call troops to battle. It's what Paul was referring to in 1 Corinthians 14:8: "If the trumpet makes an uncertain sound, who will prepare for battle?" Another one of its major uses was to celebrate victory over your enemies.

Psalm 89:15 says, "Blessed are the people who know the joyful sound!" This verse is referring to the sound of the shofar. This shout of victory is illustrated two times in Scripture. First, we saw it when the people of Israel surrounded the city of Jericho and marched around it, and then they blew the shofar and gave a mighty shout—and the walls came tumbling down.

Second, we will hear the shofar blast and a shout of victory on the day of the Rapture of the church.

> For the Lord Himself will descend from heaven with a shout, with the voice of an archangel, and *with the trumpet of God.* And the dead in Christ will rise first. Then we who are alive and remain shall be caught up together with them in the clouds to meet the Lord in the air. And thus we shall always be with the Lord.
>
> —1 THESSALONIANS 4:16–17

The Bible says Jesus will descend from heaven with a shout. What is that shout about? That shout is victory—it is victory over death, hell, and the grave. Because when every ounce of your physical body has been taken out of that grave He becomes the total victor over death, hell and the grave—and He is shouting for His victory!

The blast from the shofar in this passage is called a *teruah*, which is an "awakening blast." Ephesians 5:14 says, "*Awake*, you who sleep, arise from the dead, and Christ will give you light."

Many Christians believe that the concept of resurrection began in the New Testament. Not so! The Old Testament is God's will concealed; the New Testament is God's will revealed. Every doctrine in the New Testament started in the Old Testament.

In the Old Testament, the prophet Isaiah describes the coming resurrection of believers: "Your dead shall live; together with my dead body they shall arise. Awake and sing, you who dwell in dust; for your dew is like the dew of herbs, and the earth shall cast out the dead" (Isaiah 26:19).

Concerning the resurrection, the Old Testament prophet Daniel said, "Many of those who sleep in the dust of the earth shall awake, some to everlasting life, some to shame and everlasting contempt" (12:2). Daniel makes it clear that there are two resurrections: there will be a resurrection of the just, and there will be a resurrection of the unjust. When Christ appears in the clouds of heaven, only the righteous will go with him.

The Feast of Trumpets is the celebration of a great victory, of a new thing. When you get saved, you become a new creation in Christ Jesus. The Bible says, "Behold, all things have become new" (2 Corinthians 5:17). Blow the shofar and shout for joy—for you have been liberated from death, hell, and the grave! You have become heirs of God and joint heirs with Jesus Christ (Romans 8:17).

That means everything He had, you have—and everything you had, He now has. He took your poverty and gave you his wealth. He took your sickness and gave you His divine health. He took the fact that you were outside the covenants of Israel and he adopted you into the family of God. He has given to you eternal life. He has given his angels charge over you to protect you. He has taken all of your debts and turned them into the riches of Abraham. You are a new creation, an ambassador of the King of kings and Lord of lords! You are royalty, so act like it and think like it and speak like it, in Jesus' name!

There are three trumpets in Scripture you need to know about:

- The *first trump* was blown at Mount Sinai, announcing the giving of the Word of God to His people, the Ten Commandments (Exodus 19:13, 19).
- The *last trump* is in 1 Corinthians 15:51–52. This trumpet is blown at the Rapture of the church, when the church is taken from the earth and arises to meet Christ in the air.
- The final trump is the *great trump*, described in Matthew 24:31. The great trump will be blown at the Second Coming of Christ.

There are some who teach that the church will go through the Great Tribulation because the only place in the Bible they can find a series of trumpets is in the book of Revelation, so they think the "last trumpet" is the one that happens in the book of Revelation. Listen to me: the church is not going through the Tribulation, not five minutes of it!

There are three trumpets. The first trump is sounded at Sinai. The last trump sounds at the Rapture of the church. The great trump sounds at the feast of Yom Kippur, which is the Second Coming.

The church is *not* going through the Tribulation! God did not save us to let the Antichrist torment us—how foolish is that?

The Feast of Trumpets is the rehearsal for the Rapture. "They will see the Son of Man coming on the clouds of heaven with power and great glory. And He will send His angels with a great sound of a trumpet, and they will gather together His elect from the four winds, from one end of heaven to the other" (Matthew 24:30–31).

Put these verses together and you have this picture. Jesus is the Prince of Glory who appears suddenly in the heavens. It will be a brilliant demonstration of light. "As the lightning comes from the east and flashes to the west, so also will the coming of the Son of Man be" (Matthew 24:27). Then the trump of God (the shofar) will sound, announcing the appearance of royalty, because he is the Prince of Peace, the King of kings, the Lord of lords.

On the day of the Rapture, the voice of the archangel will summon the righteous dead from their graves, and all over the earth the graves will explode as the righteous occupants who are there soar to the heavens. The marble mausoleums will shatter as they rise to meet the Lord in the air. Cars will be parked along the highway, the motors still running, the driver and occupants strangely missing, because now they have been transferred from streets of asphalt to streets of gold. Homes of believers will have the supper dishes on the table, the food is on the stove but the occupants have risen to the marriage supper of the lamb prepared by God the Father for the bride of Jesus Christ without spot or wrinkle.

Headlines will be screaming in the newspaper, "Millions are missing!" Cameras will go from cemetery to cemetery filming the empty graves, ruptured mausoleums, empty homes, empty cars. If you're not saved, don't dare fly with a Christian pilot—he's going up and you're going down! It's going to be exciting. Newscasters will try to explain what is going on. New Agers will be jabbering about arrival of spaceships. Telephone lines will be jammed with loved ones trying to reach us—but we will be out of range, in the city where the Lamb is the light!

Churches are going to be packed with weeping, hysterical people who know the Lord has come and they have been left behind to go through the Great Tribulation. They were religious, but they were lost. They went to church, but they never accepted Jesus Christ. They knew all the buzzwords, but they didn't have the Lord of glory or the blood of the cross on the doorposts of their soul. Ready or not, He is coming—and He's coming soon!

If you don't believe in the Rapture as described in the Bible, where people rise to meet the Lord in the air, how are you going to know when the real Jesus gets here? Anyone can stand on the Mount of Olives and claim to be Jesus. Anyone can wear a white robe. Anyone can be a descendant of King David. Anyone can have his followers crown him as the king of the New Israel in Jerusalem. He can surgically have scars put into his hands and his feet. That can be done. But this is not the real Jesus.

Jesus warns us, "If anyone says to you, 'Look, here is the Christ!' or 'There!' do not believe it" (Matthew 24:23). They are frauds; they are imposters. If you follow them, they are going to destroy your soul. Jesus said that if it were possible, even the very elect would be deceived (Matthew 24:24). If any man says, "Here is Christ" or "There is Christ," believe it not! He is seated at the right hand of God the Father, where He is going to stay until *the sound of the shofar,* when the dead in Christ shall rise, and we rise to meet the Lord in the air!

How will we know when Jesus gets here? Not by the newspaper headlines or professor or deranged personality pretending to be the king of Israel, not by some warlock trying to call fire from heaven. I'll know it's the real Jesus when I hear the sound of the trumpet and my body sails in the air and I stand in the glorious presence of the King of kings with my disease-proof body. I'll know *that's* the real Jesus!

Some people say the Bible really isn't literal; it's allegorical. An allegory is a myth. But you've never read a more literal book in your life. You can go to any library and validate the literal facts. As we saw on pages 84–85 of *Four Blood Moons,* Jesus was literally born on this earth, lived a sinless life, died, was physically resurrected, and ascended into heaven. This is not a myth! This is a fact. He is literally coming back again with power and great glory, and every knee will bow before Him and every tongue will confess that He is Lord to the glory of God the Father (Philippians 2:10–11). Believers in Christ are literally going to rise in the air. We are literally going to walk on streets of gold. We are literally going to wear a crown of life. We are literally going to live forever and forever because we are redeemed by the blood of Jesus Christ! Hallelujah to the Lamb of God.

Critics say the Rapture is nothing but escapism, that people who believe in the Rapture just want to escape from the world. Let me tell you, the Rapture is no more escapism from the world than salvation is escapism from hell itself. I gladly tell you that Jesus is my Savior and heaven is my home. I'm thrilled that I'm not going to the lake of fire. If that's escapism, then hallelujah, bring it on!

In Luke 21:36, Jesus said, "Watch therefore, and pray always that you may be counted worthy to escape all these things that will come to pass, and to stand before the Son of Man." The Bible very clearly teaches that if you are not watching, you are not going. That's very important. "How shall we escape if we neglect so great a salvation . . . ?" (Hebrews 2:3).

Jesus is the answer for your eternal salvation! The Feast of Trumpets reminds us that He is coming soon to rapture His church—are you ready?

THE FEAST OF ATONEMENT—*YOM KIPPUR*
(Future Fulfillment: The Second Coming)

Yom Kippur is the most holy and sacred day in the Jewish year. In biblical times, it was the only occasion on which the high priest could enter the Holy of Holies:

> Also the tenth day of this seventh month shall be the Day of Atonement. It shall be a holy convocation for you; you shall afflict your souls, and offer an offering made by fire to the LORD. And you shall do no work on that same day, for it *is* the Day of Atonement, to make atonement for you before the LORD your God.
>
> —LEVITICUS 23:27–28

On this singular day in Israel the high priest would bring a bull and two goats to the altar as the sin offering. First, the bull was sacrificed to purge the temple of the sins committed by the priest or any member of this house.

Next, the two goats were brought to the altar for sacrifice. One goat was sacrificed as an offering to purge the temple of sins committed by the people of Israel. It was the required sacrifice for national repentance as mandated in Leviticus 16:15. The first goat was slaughtered on the spot, and its blood was poured into a bowl. Then the high priest would put his thumb and his forefinger into the bowl of blood and mark the forehead of the second goat. This second goat was called the scapegoat. The scapegoat was then taken out into the wilderness and thrown over a cliff to die. When the scapegoat died, the national sins of Israel were forgiven.

Jesus is our sacrifice. The Feast of Atonement foreshadowed the blood atonement and the eternal life that we have through Jesus in the cross. Isaiah describes this exactly in Isaiah 53:4: "Surely He has *borne* our griefs and *carried* our sorrows; yet we esteemed Him stricken, smitten by God, and afflicted."

Notice those words *borne* and *carried*. Our sins were placed upon Jesus at the cross, and then He carried them away, like the scapegoat. God the Father dipped his thumb and forefinger in the blood of Jesus Christ and placed upon His head our sin. And when Jesus died, your sins, though they were crimson, became white as snow, buried in the deepest sea, never to be remembered against you anymore.

Interestingly, rabbinical scholars state that during the ceremony with the two goats, a crimson sash would be tied to the door of the Temple. At the moment that the scapegoat was released into the wilderness and died (as witnessed by the rabbi who took him out there), the red sash on the temple door would turn white. It was a sign from God that Israel's sin had been totally forgiven.

According to Jewish tradition, forty years *before* the destruction of the Temple, the sash stopped turning white. Why? Because forty years before the destruction of the Temple in AD 70, Jesus died on the cross and it was the final sacrifice required for our sin, which meant there was no longer a need to have a scapegoat. Your sins, once and for all, were paid for and forgiven by the shed blood of Jesus Christ. Now when you ask for forgiveness in the name of Jesus Christ, heaven takes the blood of the Lamb and washes your record clean. It is spotless, buried, and never to be remembered anymore!

The blood of Jesus Christ is precious because the blood of bulls and goats cannot save you. Only the blood of the Son of God can cleanse you from your sins. You're not saved by humanitarian kindness or philanthropy. You're only saved by the precious blood of the Son of God. You can only be saved when you go to the cross and invite Christ to be your substitutionary sacrifice. He is the only One who bore your sins and carried them away. You will then be part of the resurrection day when the trump of God will sound and you will rise up to meet the Son of God in all of His glory!

The blood of Jesus is the only way to salvation. I've heard lots of secular professors say we are all on the same road going to the same place. Wrong! The Bible clearly states that without the shedding of blood, there is no remission of sins (Hebrews 9:22). *Only* the blood will save you. There's no other fountain, there's no other source—nothing but the blood of Jesus!

And this same Jesus, who came to earth the first time as the Lamb of God slain for our sins, will return to earth as the conquering King in an event that will usher in a day of unprecedented national repentance.

The Feast of Trumpets foreshadows the Rapture of the church—the moment when Christ returns in the clouds in an instant to gather His church and remove believers from the earth before the Great Tribulation. But the Bible reveals that Jesus will also appear on earth a second time, and it is consistent with Scripture to say that His Second Coming could be at the Feast of Atonement.

When Christ returns at His Second Coming, He will come down from heaven with the armies of heaven and set His foot on the Mount of Olives. He will win a dramatic victory over the Battle of Armageddon in Israel. As a result, the Jewish people will finally understand who Jesus is and recognize Him as their Messiah. The Jews will mourn over their sins, they will turn to God, and in that moment, they will be saved (Romans 11:26; Zechariah 12:10–11; 13:6). It will be the greatest day of national repentance the nation of Israel has ever experienced!

Then, with joy and compassion, on that great and glorious fulfillment of the Feast of Atonement, Jesus will at last gather His chosen people to Himself.

FEAST OF TABERNACLES—SUKKOT
(Future Fulfillment: The Millennial Kingdom)

We conclude our study of the prophecy of the seven feasts with this final feast. Why should you be concerned about the Feast of

Tabernacles? Because in the millennial reign we are going to celebrate the Feast of Tabernacles every year in the city of Jerusalem.

We examined the prophetic significance of the Feast of Tabernacles on pages 179–81 of *Four Blood Moons*. There, we learned that the Feast of Tabernacles is a time of remembrance, rejoicing, and rest.

> You shall observe the Feast of Tabernacles seven days, when you have gathered from your threshing floor and from your winepress. And you shall rejoice in your feast, you and your son and your daughter, your male servant and your female servant and the Levite, the stranger and the fatherless and the widow, who *are* within your gates. Seven days you shall keep a sacred feast to the LORD your God in the place which the LORD chooses, because the LORD your God will bless you in all your produce and in all the work of your hands, so that you surely rejoice.
>
> —DEUTERONOMY 16:13–15

The Feast of Tabernacles is a harvest festival that represents a time of great rejoicing and thanksgiving for God's provision.

People hear the word *tabernacle* and think of a grand, massive building. But the word tabernacle used here is *sukkot,* which means "booth" or "hut." This feast is also referred to as the Feast of Booths.

Why did God command His people to live in temporary huts for seven days? To remind them that in their journey from the Red Sea to the Promised Land, the children of Israel dwelled in temporary places.

Today if you go to the nation of Israel during the Feast of Tabernacle, you will see the people have small huts on the balconies of their homes. The Jewish people will eat in them, and some will sleep in them, for a period of seven days. Why? Because it reminds them of where they have come from to where they are. Some of you need to do the same thing. You need to remember where you came from—and every day you need to thank God for bringing you to where you are today.

One of the messages of the booth is that our life here on earth is temporary. Paul uses the language of tabernacles in 2 Corinthians 5:1, where he describes this earthly body as a "tent": "We know that if our earthly house, *this tent*, is destroyed, we have a building from God, a house not made with hands, eternal in the heavens."

We are living in a temporary hut! Take care of your body, but know it's going to grow old and wither away. However, there is coming a day when we will receive a supernatural body, a disease-free body, a never-dying body, a resurrection body. That day is coming!

As I mentioned in *Four Blood Moons*, this festival is also referred to as the "Season of Our Rejoicing."

The Feast of Tabernacles follows the Feast of Atonement. The fact is, when you are forgiven of your sins, when you are cleansed from all unrighteousness through the blood of atonement, it is a time of joy! Rejoice in the Lord! I say again: rejoice! Your sins are forgiven. Your name is recorded in the Lamb's Book of Life! Hallelujah to the Lamb!

The Feast of Tabernacles is also a rehearsal dinner for the millennial reign of Jesus Christ. After the Second Coming, King Jesus will set up His throne and rule over the earth for a thousand years. He is going to rule from Jerusalem, and He will crush any nations that attack Israel. He will be victorious over all. Zechariah 14:16–17 validates that during the millennial reign the Feast of Tabernacles will be conducted once every year.

Jesus was born during the Feast of Tabernacles. His birth was a time of exceedingly great joy. The first time Jesus came, he came as a lamb. The next time Jesus comes, He will come as the Lion of the tribe of Judah. Jesus Christ was and is and always shall be King of kings and Lord of lords! The Feast of Tabernacles reminds us that someday King Jesus will rule over all the earth for a thousand years. It will be a time of unspeakable joy and full of great glory!

Frequently Asked Questions about *Four Blood Moons*

Q: Are you saying that the Rapture will occur on September 28, 2015?

A: Absolutely not! As I make unmistakably clear in the book *Four Blood Moons*, "the coming Four Blood Moons of 2014–15 does not mean the Rapture is going to happen during that time. Why? Because the Rapture could happen at any moment" (244).

As I have stated repeatedly, the Rapture of the church is imminent—it could happen before you finish reading this sentence. There is not one single prophecy that must be fulfilled before Christ comes to catch us up together with Him in the clouds. I am most certainly *not* saying that the Four Blood Moons are specifically announcing the Rapture of the church.

Q: Do the Four Blood Moons signify that the Second Coming will occur during 2014–15?

A: Not necessarily. I am not setting a time or a date for the Second Coming. The Bible says that God alone knows exactly when Jesus will return to earth: "Of that day and hour no one knows, not even the angels of heaven, but My Father only" (Matthew 24:36). No person can predict the day or the hour of Jesus' Second Coming.

I believe we can and should study biblical prophecy and be aware of signs that demonstrate that the day of His return is drawing near (Luke 21:28). However, I do not believe that I—or anyone else—can state with certainty the exact time or date of the Second Coming.

Q: If it's not the Rapture or the Second Coming, then what event will happen during the Four Blood Moons of 2014–2015? What is the "something big" that is about to happen?

A: We cannot be certain yet exactly what event God is announcing on His heavenly billboard through these Four Blood Moons. But we *can* be sure of this: a significant, world-changing event will occur that directly relates to Israel and the Jewish people. Similar to the events that occurred on earth during the Tetrads of 1492, 1949, and 1967, this coming world event will begin with tragedy and tears for the Jewish people, but it will ultimately end in triumph!

Q: Does God mention a Tetrad in Scripture? Is there any significance to the number four?

A: The Bible does not specifically mention a Tetrad, or Four Blood Moons. But in biblical prophecy, the number four often seems to indicate completion of some kind. There are *four* living creatures in Ezekiel, Daniel, and Revelation. There are *four* Horsemen of the Apocalypse. And there are *four* angels standing ready at the *four* corners of the earth.

Jesus is from the tribe of Judah, the *fourth* tribe of Israel. *Four* Gospels tell of His birth, life, death, and resurrection.

We can also see the number four featured prominently throughout God's creation. The universe consists of *four* main elements—earth, fire, air, and water. There are *four* regions of the earth—north, south, east, and west. There are *four* divisions of the day—morning, noon, evening, and midnight. And there are *four* seasons of the year—spring, summer, autumn, and winter. Interestingly, there are also *four* main phases of the moon.

So while the Bible doesn't attach a specific significance to the number of Four Blood Moons, the number four does seem consistent with other features of creation and biblical prophecy.

Q. What is the significance of the Four Blood Moons occurring in a Shemittah year?

A: The Shemittah year (also called the Sabbatical year) occurs every seventh year. Shemittah is highly significant in the Jewish calendar, because the Shemittah year is "Shabbat" (Sabbath) for the land of Israel, much like the weekly "Shabbat" (Sabbath), which occurs every seven days, is a time of rest for the people. In Leviticus 25:1–7 and Deuteronomy 15, God commands His people to observe the Shemittah year, which leads to abundance and blessing.

However, according to Jeremiah 34:12–22 and 2 Chronicles 36:15–21, neglecting the Shemittah year leads to God's judgment. In America, the judgment of violating Shemittah is not linked to the land of Israel but to our national disobedience to the Word of God. Every Shemittah year, God allows something to happen that gets our undivided attention—from *Roe v. Wade* to Hussein's invasion of Iran to the September 11 terrorist attacks.

The Four Blood Moons of 2104–15 are extremely unique in that, unlike the other three Tetrads that have occurred during the last five hundred years, the coming series of Four Blood Moons *includes a Shemittah year*! The Shemittah year begins September 25, 2014 and ends on September 13, 2015. As we have seen, God does everything at a "set time" (Psalm 102:13). It is no coincidence that the coming Four Blood Moons will appear in conjunction with the Shemittah year! Something big is about to happen!

Q: Why do you believe that the Four Blood Moons are significant to the nation of Israel?

A: According to the Bible, the sun, moon, and earth are controlled by God Almighty (Genesis 1:14). He is the One who puts them in direct alignment in a certain day. God sovereignly controls the movements of the heavenly bodies to the exact split second.

As we saw in *Four Blood Moons* and this companion study guide, the Tetrads of 1493–94, 1949–50, and 1967–68 all occurred during years that were very significant to Israel and the Jewish people. Each series of Four Blood Moons marked a significant historical event that started with tears and ended with triumph for the nation of Israel. There is zero probability that this is coincidence or a random chance.

God says, "I am the Lord, I do not change" (Malachi 3:6). He is "the same yesterday, today, and forever" (Hebrews 13:8). What God has done God will do. God does everything by a set pattern. So when we look back over the past five hundred years and see that every time a Tetrad of Blood Moons happened there was a major world event affecting the Jews, it is clear that the common denominator of the Four Blood Moons is Israel and the Jewish people. Because God never changes, we have to say logically that the coming Four Blood Moons will also signify an event that involves the nation of Israel.

I believe that in these next two years we are going to see something dramatic happen in the Middle East involving Israel that will change the course of history in the Middle East and impact the entire world. I believe we are seeing the genesis of that by America as a nation separating itself from Israel. For the first time in American history, we have leadership that is putting daylight between Jerusalem and Washington. I believe we are setting into motion a series of events that will change the course of world history. (For more information about biblical prophecy concerning these end-times events, see chapter 13.)

Regardless of what specific world event will occur during the Four Blood Moons of 2014–15, it is clear that it will be something that affects Israel and the Jewish people. God is showing us that something significant is going to happen—specifically related to the nation of Israel—that will cause the world to change forever!

Q: Where can I find out more about the coming Tetrad of Four Blood Moons?

A: First, read the book *Four Blood Moons: Something Is about to Change* and complete the exercises in this companion study guide and journal. Then, for additional teaching about the 2014–15 Four Blood Moons, watch or listen to my sermon series *The Coming Four Blood Moons: Something Is about to Change* and the *Four Blood Moons* studio teaching, which are available at JHM.org. I also encourage you to do your own research online, starting with NASA's website (www.NASA.gov), comparing the data and projections from esteemed scientists with the information you have learned through *Four Blood Moons* and this companion study guide and journal.

Are You Ready?

As we close this companion study guide and journal, I want to ask you a simple—but very important—question. *Are you ready?* Because the Bible says that no one knows the day or the hour that Jesus Christ could come.

Here's what we know for sure: When a major celestial event has happened only three times in over five hundred years, this is a massive demonstration from the heavens. All of the dates given by NASA for the Tetrads of Four Blood Moons in recent history— 1492, 1949, 1967—relate to the Jewish people and Israel.

We are about to receive another sign from God.

When very credible science agrees with the very credible prophet Joel and Saint Peter in the book of Acts—and I don't think that in my lifetime I've seen a more obvious demonstration of the unity of those two ingredients—we know that something big is about to happen. We may not be here to see it. The church may already be gone in the Rapture. Or the church may see this and be taken after. But one thing is for sure: the best scientific minds in the world are saying the Four Blood Moons are going to happen, and the best prophetic voices in the Word have said this is what it looks like when it happens.

Based on all I know about the Bible, and I have studied it every day for fifty-four years, there's not one thing that has to happen before the Rapture . . . we're out of here. Jesus says, "When you see these things begin to happen, look up and lift up your heads, because your redemption draws near" (Luke 21:28).

So I'm asking you, if Jesus Christ comes today in the clouds of heaven for His people, are you ready to stand before Him in the day of judgment? Is there anything in your life that you're doing of which you know God disapproves? If so, the Bible calls that sin, and sin will not enter into heaven. All you have to do to get it off your record is to confess it. God says if you confess your sins to Him, then He will bury them in the sea of forgetfulness and He will remember your sins no more.

If you know there's something in your life you need to ask forgiveness for, I want to pray with you that it will be well between you and the Lord:

Heavenly Father,

In the authority of Jesus' name, I ask You to forgive me of all of my sin. Cleanse me from all ungodliness. Let everything in my life that displeases You be removed by the blood of Jesus Christ.

And now, because Jesus is Lord and I have confessed my sins, the Lord is removing them from my record in heaven forever. I am now a child of God, committed to serving Him with all of my mind, heart, soul, and body.

In Jesus' name, amen.

Notes

1. *Week 1:* **Does God Speak through the Heavens?**
1. Adapted from Walter A. Elwell, *Evangelical Dictionary of Theology* (Grand Rapids, MI: Baker Academic, 2001), s.v. "Jerusalem."
2. Adapted from James Orr, *International Standard Bible Encyclopedia* (Peabody, MA: Hendrickson, 1994), s.v. "watchman," http://www.internationalstandardbible.com/W/watchman.html.
3. Adapted from Strong's KJV Concordance, 226, s.v. "oth," http://biblehub.com/hebrew/strongs_226.htm.

2. *Week 2:* **Signs and Stars**
1. John Phillips, *Exploring Genesis: An Expository Commentary* (Grand Rapids: Kregel, 2001), 38.
2. Conversions from the Jewish calendar to the Western calendar are widely available online. This version was adapted from Mitchell G. Bard, "The Jewish Calendar: An Overview," Jewish Virtual Library: A Project of the American-Israeli Cooperative Enterprise, accessed June 6, 2014, http://www.jewishvirtuallibrary.org/jsource/Judaism/calendar.html. Because the corresponding dates fluctuate slightly from year to year, many websites feature exact Jewish date converters for specific Western dates.
3. Some information in this section adapted from Strong's KJV Concordance, 8059, s.v. "shemittah," http://biblehub.com/hebrew/8059.htm.

3. *Week 3:* **End-Times Prophecy**

1. Some information from this section adapted from "Temple of Herod," *1906 Jewish Encyclopedia,* JewishEncyclopedia.com, http://www.jewishencyclopedia.com/articles/14304-temple-of-herod. For more detailed information on Herod's Temple, see "Temple, A2," *International Standard Bible Encyclopedia,* BibleStudyTools.com, http://www.biblestudytools.com/encyclopedias/isbe/temple-a2.html.

5. *Week 5:* **The Beginning of the End**

1. Adapted from John Hagee, "The Church of Laodecea," *7 Letters of the Apocalypse, vol. 2,* http://www.jhm.org/Catalog/Product/1142/TheChurchOfLaodicea. Definition of *anarchy* from Merriam-Webster, Merriam-Webster.com, definition 1b, http://www.merriam-webster.com/dictionary/anarchy.

8. *Week 8:* **The Four Blood Moons of 1967–68 and 2014–15**

1. Definition of *terminal* from Merriam-Webster, Merriam-Webster.com, definition 3a, http://www.merriam-webster.com/dictionary/terminal.

Sources Referenced

Hagee, John. "Prophecy of Atonement." *Prophecy of the Seven Feasts* DVD. San Antonio, TX: John Hagee Ministries, 2013.

Hagee, John. "Prophecy of Tabernacles." *Prophecy of the Seven Feasts* DVD. San Antonio, TX: John Hagee Ministries, 2013.

Hagee, John. "The Feast of Trumpets." *Prophecy of the Seven Feasts* DVD. San Antonio, TX: John Hagee Ministries, 2013.

Hagee, John. "Why Christians Should Support Israel." John Hagee Ministries. http://www.jhm.org/Home/About/WhySupportIsrael.

Hagee, John. *Can America Survive?: 10 Prophetic Signs That We Are the Terminal Generation.* Brentwood, TN: Howard, 2010.

Hagee, John. *Four Blood Moons Studio Teaching* CD. San Antonio, TX: John Hagee Ministries, 2013.

Hagee, John. *Four Blood Moons: Something Is about to Change.* Brentwood, TN: Worthy, 2013.

Hagee, John. *His Glory Revealed: A Devotional.* Nashville: Thomas Nelson, 1999.

Hagee, John. *Jerusalem Countdown, Revised and Updated: A Prelude to War.* Lake Mary, FL: Frontline, 2013.

Hagee, John. *The Battle for Jerusalem.* Nashville: Thomas Nelson, 2013.

Hagee, John. *The Coming Four Blood Moons* DVD, parts 1–3. San Antonio, TX: John Hagee Ministries, 2013.

Hagee, John. *The Genesis of the Four Blood Moons: Interview with Pastor John Hagee* DVD. San Antonio, TX: John Hagee Ministries, 2013.

WORTHY®
PUBLISHING

If you enjoyed this book, will you consider
sharing the message with others?

- Mention the book in a Facebook post, Twitter update,
  Pinterest pin, blog post, or upload a picture through
  Instagram.

- Recommend this book to those in your small group,
  book club, workplace, and classes.

- Head over to facebook.com/worthypublishing, "LIKE" the
  page, and post a comment as to what you enjoyed the most.

- Tweet "I recommend reading #FourBloodMoonsStudyGuide
  by @PastorJohnHagee // @worthypub"

- Pick up a copy for someone you know who would be
  challenged and encouraged by this message.

- Write a book review online.

You can subscribe to Worthy Publishing's newsletter at
www.worthypublishing.com

WORTHY PUBLISHING
FACEBOOK PAGE

WORTHY PUBLISHING
WEBSITE